Japanese Genre Painting

1. *The Hikone Screen (detail). Entire screen shown in Plate 88.* See note, page 144.

Japanese Genre Painting
The Lively Art
of Renaissance Japan

BY **Kondo Ichitaro**

Curator, Reference Materials, Tokyo National Museum

TRANSLATED BY **Roy Andrew Miller**

CHARLES E. TUTTLE COMPANY: PUBLISHERS

Rutland, Vermont & Tokyo, Japan

European Representative

BOXERBOOKS, INC., Zurich

Published by the Charles E. Tuttle Company
of Rutland, Vermont & Tokyo, Japan,
with editorial offices at
15 Edogawa-cho, Bunkyo-ku, Tokyo
© 1961, by the Charles E. Tuttle Co.
Library of Congress Catalog
Card No. 60–15605
First printing, 1961

Printed in Japan

Contents

LIST OF PLATES   *page*   9

INTRODUCTION   *page* 11

    The Beginnings: A Japanese Renaissance?

    A Changing Japanese Society

    The New Art

    Genre Painting

PLATES   *page* 29

NOTES ON THE PLATES   *page* 135

List of Plates

1. The Hikone Screen (detail). National Treasure. Coll. Ii Naochika: 4
2. Genre Painting Screen (detail). Coll. Tokyo National Museum: 31
3. Kano Naganobu: Pleasures under the Blossoms (detail). National Treasure. Coll. Hara Kunizo: 33
4. The River Bed at Shijo (detail). Important Cultural Property. Coll. Seika-do: 35
5. The Pleasures of Women (detail). Important Art Object. Coll. Yahata Yotaro: 37
6. Honda Heihachiro Portrait Screen (detail). Important Cultural Property. Coll. Reimei-kai: 39
7. Dancing Figures (detail). Important Art Object. Coll. City of Kyoto: 41
8. Bath Women. Important Cultural Property. Coll. Atami Museum of Fine Art: 43
9. The "Nun." Coll. Atami Museum of Fine Art: 45
10. Kaigetsu-do Ando: Courtesan. Coll. Takeuchi Kimpei: 47
11-15. Customs of the Twelve Months. Important Art Object. Coll. Yamaguchi Hoshun: 49-51
16-23. Genre Painting Screen. Coll. Tokyo National Museum: 50-51
24. Kano Hideyori: Autumn-Foliage Viewing at Takao. National Treasure. Coll. Tokyo National Museum: 52-53
25-26. Views in and around Kyoto. Important Cultural Property. Coll. Machida Mitsujiro: 54-55
27-28. Kano Eitoku: Views in and around Kyoto. Important Cultural Property. Coll. Uesugi Takanori: 56-59
29-32. Famous Places in Kyoto. Coll. anonymous: 60-63
33-34. Genre Painting Mounted on Sliding Doors. Important Cultural Property. Coll. Emman-in: 64-65
35-36. Genre Painting Mounted on Sliding Doors of Audience Chamber in Nagoya Castle. Important Cultural Property. Coll. City of Nagoya: 66-67
37-38. Festival Ceremonies at the Toyokuni Shrine. Important Art Object. Coll. Reimei-kai: 68-71
39-40. Kano Naizen: Festival Ceremonies at the Toyokuni Shrine. Important Cultural Property. Coll. Toyokuni Shrine: 72-75
41-44. Views of Artisans. Coll. Okazoe Misao: 76
45-49. Kano Yoshinobu: Views of Artisans. Important Cultural Property. Coll. Kita-in: 77-78
50-52. Flower Viewing and Falconry. Important Art Object. Coll. Atami Museum of Fine Art: 79-81
53. Kano Naganobu: Pleasures under the Blossoms. National Treasure. Coll Hara Kunizo: 82-83
54-55. Tethered Horses. Important Art Object. Coll. Tokyo National Museum: 84-85
56-57. Screen with Equestrian Figures. Important Cultural Property Coll. Daigo-ji: 86-87
58-59. A Dog-Baiting Meet. Important Cultural Property. Coll. Sugawara Tsusai: 88-89
60-61. Festival Ceremonies at the Kamo Shrine. Important Cultural Property. Coll. anonymous: 90-91
62-63. "Southern Barbarians" Screen. Coll. Tokyo National Museum: 92-93
64-65. "Southern Barbarians" Screen. Coll. Kobayashi Chu: 92-93
66-68. The River Bed at Shijo. Important Cultural Property. Coll. Seika-do: 94-98
69. The River Bed at Shijo (detail). Important Cultural Property. Coll. Domoto Shiro: 99
70. The River Bed at Shijo. Coll. Misumi Kazunari: 100-1
71. The River Bed at Shijo. Important Cultural Property. Coll. Domoto Shiro: 100-1
72. The Kiyomizu Temple. Important Art Object. Coll. Atami Museum of Fine Art: 102-3
73. Screen with Kabuki Scene. Important Art Object. Coll. Yamamoto Kiyo-o: 102-3
74-75. Screen with Kabuki Scene. Important Art Object. Coll. Otsuga Zenin: 104-5
76-77. Hishikawa Moronobu (?): Screen with Kabuki Scene. Important Art Object. Coll. Tokyo National Museum: 106-9
78. Kabuki Sketchbook Scroll (detail). Important Art Object. Coll. Reimei-kai: 110-11
79. Okuni Kabuki Scroll (detail). Important Art Object. Coll. Umehara Ryuzaburo: 110
80. Okuni Kabuki Scroll (detail). Important Art Object. Coll. Kyoto University Library: 111
81-82. The So-o-ji Screen. Important Art Object. Coll. Reimei-kai: 112-13

83. *The Weavers. Coll. Atami Museum of Fine Art: 114*
84. *The Rope Door. Important Art Object. Coll. Hara Kunizo: 115*
85. *Genre Painting. Coll. Okazaki Masaomi: 116*
86. *The Gion Festival. Coll. Tokyo National Museum: 117*
87. *Genre Screen with Female Figures. Coll. Hosomi Ryoichi: 116–17*
88. *The Hikone Screen. National Treasure. Coll. Ii Naochika: 118–19*
89. *The Pleasures of Women. Important Art Object. Coll. Yahata Yotaro: 120–21*
90. *Dancing Figures. Important Art Object. Coll. City of Kyoto: 122–23*
91. *Dancing Figure. Coll. Umehara Ryuzaburo: 122*
92. *A "Kambun Beauty." Coll. Tokyo National Museum: 122*
93-95. *Genre Figures. Coll. Nezu Museum: 123*
96. *Honda Heihachiro Portrait Screen. Important Cultural Property. Coll. Reimei-kai: 124–25*
97. *The "Pilgrim." Coll. Atami Museum of Fine Art: 126*
98. *A Bath Woman. Coll. Nakamura Gakuryo: 126*
99. *A "Kambun Beauty." Coll. Ujiie Takeo: 127*
100. *Dancing Courtesan? Coll. Tokyo National Museum: 127*
101. *Male Dancer. Coll. Atami Museum of Fine Art: 127*
102. *Okumura Masanobu: The Ogura Mountain Villa. Coll. Tokyo National Museum: 128*
103. *Hishikawa Moronobu: Beauty Looking over Her Shoulder. Coll. Tokyo National Museum: 128*
104. *Torii Kiyonobu: Beauty with Umbrella. Coll. Tokyo National Museum: 128*
105. *Nishikawa Sukenobu: Beauty at Her Toilet. Coll. Atami Museum of Fine Art: 129*
106. *Tosen-do Rifu: Standing Beauty. Coll. Tokyo National Museum: 129*
107. *Miyagawa Choki: Courtesan Enjoying Incense. Coll. Tokyo National Museum: 129*
108. *Miyagawa Choshun: Female Figure. Important Art Object. Coll. Yamato Bunka-kan: 130*
109. *Miyagawa Choshun: Courtesan Enjoying Incense. Coll. Tokyo National Museum: 130*
110. *Hishikawa Moronobu: Genre Scroll (detail). Coll. Tokyo National Museum: 131*
111. *Miyagawa Choshun: Genre Scroll (detail). Coll. Tokyo National Museum: 131*
112-15. *Iwasa Katsumochi: The Thirty-six Poets. Important Cultural Property. Coll. Tosho-gu: 132*
116. *The Horie Romance Scroll (detail). Coll. Atami Museum of Fine Art: 133*
117. *Lady Tokiwa Scroll (detail). Coll. Atami Museum of Fine Art: 133*
118. *The Oguri Hangan Romance Scroll (detail). Coll. The Imperial Family: 133*
119. *The Princess Joruri Romance Scroll (detail). Coll. Atami Museum of Fine Art: 133*

TEXT ILLUSTRATIONS

FIG. 1. Detail from "Views in and around Kyoto" by Kano Eitoku: 10
FIG. 2. Detail from "Southern Barbarians" Screen: 11
FIG. 3. Detail from "Festival Ceremonies at the Toyokuni Shrine": 14
FIG. 4. Detail from "Festival Ceremonies at the Toyokuni Shrine" by Kano Naizen: 15
FIG. 5. Detail from "Genre Painting Screen": 17
FIG. 6. Detail from "Views in and around Kyoto" by Kano Eitoku: 19
FIG. 7. Detail from "The River Bed at Shijo": 22
FIG. 8. Detail from "The River Bed at Shijo": 24

Introduction

1. THE BEGINNINGS: A JAPANESE RENAISSANCE?

The period of Japanese cultural history reaching roughly from the sixteenth to the seventeenth centuries is often compared to Renaissance Europe, while some authorities have preferred instead a comparison with the so-called "Medieval Renaissance" of the thirteenth century. But comparisons between Japan and Europe, which differ radically in culture as well as in their political and economic conditions, are dangerous in the extreme, especially when they consist simply of setting one group of data down alongside the other.

The four or five decades from about the middle of the fifteenth century down to the early part of the sixteenth saw certain developments in Japan which completely altered the face both of Japanese society and of Japanese culture. In the political sphere, this was the period during which the foundations were laid for the system of feudal society which was to dominate Japan for several centuries to follow, and this establishment of feudalism meant that every political vestige of the earlier stages of Japanese society had to be destroyed.

Elsewhere in the society there were also far-reaching changes. The Buddhist church, grown fat and rich over centuries of a continuous tradition of faith, was soon to have its claws pared. In its place Japan was to see the cult of Confucianism growing into a position of greater and greater prominence. In Confucianism Japan was to have a system that, at least compared to Buddhism, placed a relatively high value upon a rational approach to the things of daily life and its experiences.

Nor was this all. Commerce and communications were opened with Europe, notably with Portugal, and soon trade was flourishing. As commerce of this sort began to hit its real stride, the economic influence and position of the persons most concerned with it were of course also enhanced. These persons were of the officially despised class of commoners, and their growing economic position tended more and more to give them a zest and an enthusiasm for living that they had conspicuously lacked up to this time. Their economic liberation, for that is what really transpired, brought about an amazingly sudden development in the arts, reaching out eventually into every imaginable area of creative activity in Japan.

The Japanese Renaissance, then, if we are to admit that one took place, centered around several different phenomena. All were important and interconnected, but each produced different developments in the arts.

We have already mentioned most of the important factors; they may be summed up as the denial of the tradition of the past, the establishment of a new feudal state, the development of trade, and finally the economic liberation of the lower classes. The present volume is concerned with a fairly detailed presentation of the changes and developments in the arts which these Renaissance-causing factors brought about; but before they can be inspected in detail a closer look at the social situation which brought them about is necessary.

We began above by simply referring to the period from the sixteenth to the first part of the seventeenth century as if it formed a naturally demarcated unit, but this of course is far from the fact. There are major differences between the fairly neat divisions into periods and eras which we can make in more or less routine historical investigation and those necessary in a general cultural history, especially one that attempts to include something about the fine arts. If our point of view were merely that of the general historian, it would be simple

FIG. 1. Detail from "Views in and around Kyoto" (Plate 27) by Kano Eitoku
Kyoto, among other cities, grew rapidly in the latter half of the 16th century. This detail captures the lively bustle of the plebeian populace of the day. Note the group of court nobles engaged in the popular "foot ball" in the upper right corner. See page 13, also caption to Plates 27 & 28.

enough to state that for our purposes Japan's feudal period begins to take shape in the year 1573, thanks to the action of a single heroic figure, Oda Nobunaga, who begins to subdue existing military opposition at that time in order to unify the country. This unification of Japan was continued and finally accomplished by Oda's successor Toyotomi Hideyoshi, who died in 1598, at which point we could quite simply say that Japan's feudal society had been formed. Viewed in this fashion, the whole process could be neatly put into a twenty-five year compartment.

But cultural history, by its very nature, is not something that can be thus neatly determined by the actions of any one man. It goes its own way, at times tending to operate rather independently of political history. The "lively" tendencies in Japanese painting with which the present volume is concerned can be observed to be active as early as 1550, and they continue to be important down to as late as 1660. Thus it is very nearly a chronological century which is our concern when we speak of the Japanese Renaissance and its art.

The present volume is especially concerned with the development and growth of genre painting during this period. This is due to several reasons. One of the important ones is the fact that in this early genre painting we can detect the ultimate sources which in due time gave birth to the *ukiyo-e* print. This is still probably the one variety of Japanese art best known to the West, and one of which Japan today also appreciates the real worth. But genre painting will not be our only concern; attention is also due the significance of the decorative arts which so lavishly decorated the castles and residences of the warriors and other upper-class families of the period.

II. A CHANGING JAPANESE SOCIETY

For many centuries Japanese political life had been a complicated affair. The emperor remained on his throne, sacred and inviolable, but he almost always could be observed to be reigning instead of ruling. The actual power of the state had by long tradition come to be exercised not by the imperial throne but by certain nobles and especially by the warrior class. Down to about the middle of the twelfth century the powerful Fujiwara family of court nobles was in charge of the affairs of state; afterward they were succeeded in succes-

FIG. 2. Detail from "Southern Barbarians" Screen (Plate 65)
The flourishing foreign trade of the latter decades of the 16th century brought many a foreigner to Japan's cities, inspiring the unique genre of "Southern Barbarian" paintings. This scene is a typical detail, showing a group of representative foreigners. See page 12, also caption to Plates 64 & 65.

sion by the military clans of the Genji, the Hojo, and the Ashikaga. These exercised their political power through the originally military institution known as the *bakufu*, which became in effect the sole government of the country.

The disastrous Onin War which broke out in 1467 showed up the essential weakness of the Ashikaga *bakufu* with merciless clarity. For almost a century following this, Japan was torn apart by continual internal strife. Rebels and bandits were everywhere, and the political situation was totally beyond control. Up until about 1530 local petty lords and the often equally powerful landed families were able to capture for themselves a good deal of the actual power of the state, but in the half century following they again lost most of it, and soon found themselves being replaced on the scene by their own vassals and tenants. Japanese social structure had once more regenerated itself by the curious metabolism-like process which it had often employed in the past. Meanwhile, the Ashikaga *bakufu* found itself totally powerless to take any effective countermeasures, and during the entire twenty-five-year period from 1521 to 1546 that the thirteenth Ashikaga shogun Yoshiharu was in office he was never once able to take up residence in Kyoto, the city that was supposed to be his capital.

It was under circumstances of this sort that the powerful local *daimyo*—really little more than war lords at this point—began to make themselves heard. One such, in the vicinity of Nagoya, was Oda Nobunaga. Employing a variety of stratagems and devices he managed to pacify the troubled nation, and in 1563 was able to effect an entry into the ancient imperial capital of Kyoto, marching up from Gifu and taking with him Yoshiaki, the last of the Ashikaga shoguns. Nobunaga's entry into Kyoto was of course full of political meaning. Kyoto was the residence of the emperor, the symbol of the entire nation, and for Nobunaga to be able to exercise the reins of government from Kyoto meant that at last the whole Japanese nation had again been reunited under one ruler.

Nobunaga continued his work of unification and pacification by first bringing together his own home-ground, equivalent to present-day Aichi and Gifu prefectures (the central part of Honshu, the main island of the Japanese archipelago), and the Kyoto region, and then by extending his military power outward from these. As his enemies were driven further and further back their lands too entered under his direct military control, while his personal power by the same token grew by leaps and bounds. His forces as a matter of principle occupied all the lands they took, and in short time became the paramount political forces in the areas they occupied. The local authorities and leading families had to give way to these new military rulers, while other important areas were directly annexed. Thus Nobunaga's work of bringing all Japan under his own personal rule went on.

Opposition soon came from a not totally unexpected source—the Buddhist clergy. From the strongholds of their mighty temples, especially the rich Enryaku-ji of Mt. Hiei, near Kyoto, where they controlled thousands of willing warrior-monks in addition to vast treasures of money and lands, the Buddhist clergy were able to join in an effective opposition to Nobunaga's work of unification. He in turn was quick to strike them down. Their holy temples were mostly burnt to the ground, the proud Enryaku-ji among them. Nobunaga's opposition to Buddhism was of course not primarily a religious one—he thought of it simply in terms of the large numbers of armed men which the powerful temples were able to put into the field against him. It was this military potential of the Buddhist establishment which chiefly determined his opposition to it.

In 1582 Nobunaga set out to engage the Mori clan in battle; the Moris were powerful local rulers in the area of present-day Hiroshima. On the way he stopped for the night at the Honno-ji in Kyoto, and was assassinated as he slept there by one of his subalterns, Akechi Mitsuhide. Another subaltern, Toyotomi Hideyoshi by name, soon defeated Mitsuhide, and came in turn to lead Nobunaga's forces in completing their work of the unification of the country. It is of course this Hideyoshi who is remembered in history as the military and political successor to Nobunaga, for it was Hideyoshi who managed successfully to complete the mission upon which Nobunaga had earlier set out. In 1583 Hideyoshi became master of Kyoto, in fact as well as in name, and Japan was once again one nation.

Just forty years before Hideyoshi entered Kyoto in triumph, in 1548, a Portuguese castaway washed ashore on the island of Tanegashima in southern Japan. He had been lost from a Chinese junk on which he was taking passage. After receiving food and drink he again went on his way, but he left behind him something that was to work important changes in Japanese society—a gun of Portuguese manufacture. The possession of knowledge concerning Western firearms gave a major advantage to the local rulers of the south of Japan for some time, and later the skillful use of locally manufactured reproductions of foreign weapons was one important factor in the eventual triumph of Nobunaga and Hideyoshi.

In 1548 St. Francis Xavier landed at Kagoshima on the southernmost extremity of the island of Kyushu. This priest of the Society of Jesus was on his way from Goa, in India, and had been directed to Japan by a Japanese convert known in the records only as Angello. Opposition to Xavier's missionary activities were, however, soon expressed on the part of the Shimazu's, the local rulers of the area and devoted Buddhists, and so the Jesuit missionary and his party departed for the port of Hirado to continue their evangelical work there.

A profound and, at this present vantage point in history, very important relationship existed between the Portuguese merchants and traders of the period and the Christian missionaries in the Far East. The missionaries were the vanguard of the traders; eager in their mission of evangelization they rapidly pushed ahead, carrying their gospel into ever new lands and in among strange local faiths. But next came the traders, invariably making full use of the new gospel once it had been preached. Portugal was in effect advancing into the Far East under a banner with the brave device, "For Spice and the Holy Spirit!"

Even so, there was nothing this profound to the opposition voiced by the Shimazu family to Xavier and his mission. And for their pains in opposing him the Shimazu's were treated to a disappointing spectacle. The Portuguese merchantmen, with their valuable cargoes of cannon and firearms, as well as their fascinating and curious stores of wonderful rarities from the West, simply heaved anchor and departed with the saintly Jesuit in tow—all going off to the "enemy port" of Hirado. In the military situation of the day, new weapons were the most important consideration for every local ruler. To get one's hands on the new Portuguese weapons—the wonderful guns and the powerful cannon—it was to be necessary to permit the propagation of Christianity within one's domains. One would even find it necessary eventually to assist the missionaries in their work of evangelization by, for example, granting them lands on which they might erect their churches.

The result naturally was that a large number of local rulers in Japan outwardly made a great show of their adherence to the new Christian faith; but the real reason for their sudden conversion was clearly their desire to acquire the powerful and often decisive new weapons which their Portuguese friends would then turn over to them.

Nobunaga and Hideyoshi are surely to be counted among those who attempted in this fashion to make use of the Christian religion for their own secular ends.

This is of course not to deny the large number of genuine Christian conversions of the period, nor the faith, joy, and spiritual thanksgiving with which the new gospel was heard by many in Japan. Later, during days of bitter persecutions, thousands of Japanese were to die, often by cruel and horrible tortures, for their new faith, and these martyrs can hardly be understood had all these conversions been mere matters of convenience. And many local rulers too were sincerely converted—at least twenty-six such are known, including Konishi Yukinaga and Takayama Ukon.

But be that as it may, Japan was now embarked upon a process of far-reaching change. And for better or worse, this change was being effected by two very diverse factors, two things effectively symbolized by two quite disparate symbols—the guns the Portuguese brought in on their ships and the crucifixes of the new missionary religion being spread throughout the islands.

The city of Sakai near Osaka now became a center for the manufacture of Japanese replicas of the Portuguese guns, and the pieces produced there soon worked amazing changes in Japanese warfare. First must be mentioned the castles. Now, with firearms, these strongly fortified military centers well known in European history first began to figure on the Japanese scene. They began with the so-called "mountain castles" *(yamajiro)*, usually little but spots difficult of access high in the mountains fortified with earthworks and moats, but soon developed into the well-known castles of the plains with their gleaming white towers. As such they once were a well-known part of the Japanese scene, though few of them have survived later history and especially the bombings of World War II.

The first of these was Nobunaga's Azuchi Castle, built to command the topography of the Kyoto area and to ensure his successful storming of the city. It was erected in 1576. It was in this castle that Nobunaga granted audience to the missionary Organtino Gnecci, and here also that he gave him permission to engage in his evangelical work within his domains. This soaring castle had been located here essentially from military considerations, of course, but it was far more than merely a military stronghold. Its site made it possible to control the communications and indeed even the whole economic life of the area. Around it clustered in time the villas and residences of important officers and subalterns in Nobunaga's forces, and here too gathered the tradesmen and artisans who made the colorful way of life of their betters possible.

The whole was an integrated social and cultural unit, the first of many such to come, styled the *joka-machi*, literally "towns about the castles." In other words, they were satellite communities surrounding the increasingly important castles which were soon to dot the countryside. And the castles, as well as the colorful life in the surrounding satellite communities, owed their existence to Portuguese firearms.

The merchants and artisans in these satellite communities gradually grew in economic prestige, which growth was followed of course by a corresponding elevation in their standard of living. As they began to participate more and more in the total society of the day they made an increasingly important contribution to the cultural history of Japan, a contribution which is especially striking in the field of the fine arts. The art of what is commonly called the Momoyama period (1573–1614) was in large measure due to their efforts and taste.

Thus, Christianity in Japan received the support and adherence of important local rulers from Nobunaga on, throughout Kyushu in southern Japan as well as in the region around Kyoto and Osaka, and as a result its mission of evangelization soon bore rich fruit. By 1582 it is said that there were 150,000 Christians in Japan. Nobunaga may, it is true, have been influenced in his leanings toward Christianity by his desire to hamper the influence of the Buddhist clergy, but at any rate his protection of the new faith in the areas under his control was vigorous and positive in nature. But his death was radically to change matters.

His successor Hideyoshi at first continued Nobunaga's pro-Christian policy, but then in 1587 suddenly reversed himself and issued an order absolutely banning the faith through-

FIG. 3. Detail from "Festival Ceremonies at the Toyokuni Shrine" (Plate 38)
The realistic approach and lively vitality characteristic of the genre art of the time is clearly reflected in this detail from one of two screens portraying the gay festivities held on the seventh anniversary of the death of Hideyoshi in 1604. See page 23, also caption to Plates 37 & 38.

out the country and demanding the immediate deportation of all foreign missionaries then in Japan. The reasons for his sudden action seem clear enough; like Nobunaga he had been anxious to encourage Christianity largely in order to embarrass the Buddhists and to weaken their ability to resist his efforts at the political unification of the nation. Now that this task was in the main accomplished, he began instead to fear foreign interference with his regime, and such danger now appeared to center in the missionaries and their activities. In addition, Hideyoshi was concerned with certain indications which had already appeared showing that the new Japanese Christian community was liable to exhibit opposition to the development of his new feudal society, as well as with difficulties concerning the dispatch of Japanese slaves overseas. All these factors played a part in the sudden proscription of Christianity.

But Hideyoshi's scheme was to continue foreign trade as before, in spite of the banning of Christianity. As the coming ruler of Japan, he was anxious to separate foreign trade from foreign religions, especially since he personally was profoundly interested in and involved with the former. But, as we have noted above, the circumstances of the times made this all but impossible. Foreign trade and Christianity went everywhere hand in hand and were well nigh inseparable. Hideyoshi, as a matter of fact, was to fail completely in his attempt to separate the two. The missionaries went underground, where they continued their work, and the faith of their converts if anything grew only stronger.

Hideyoshi was not the only *de facto* ruler of Japan, however, to attempt this isolation of trade from religion; his eventual successor Tokugawa Ieyasu was also to make it his policy, as was Ieyasu's heir Hidetada. In their time, however, the situation grew more complicated. The Tokugawa rulers eventually had their attention forcibly drawn to the essentially supra-national and anti-feudal characteristics of the Christian faith, with the result that their persecution of the imported religion grew more and more severe. Ieyasu and those who followed him eventually came to realize the profound impossibility of isolating trade from religion, and finally totally shut off the nation from all contact with the outside world, being willing in the last analysis to sacrifice even their precious trade with the West if that was necessary

FIG. 4. Detail from "Festival Ceremonies at the Toyokuni Shrine" (Plate 40) by Kano Naizen
This similar detail from the work of one of the masters of the traditional Kano school reveals the interesting combination of traditional techniques and the new, plebeian subject matter. See page 23, also caption to Plates 39 & 40.

in order to stamp out the Christian faith. Japan severed its relations with Europe; it was the beginning of the "Closed Country" period of her history. The year was 1636.

Thus it was that both the Christian religion and the foreign trade which accompanied it suddenly disappeared from the fabric of Japanese society, due to the severe repressive measures taken by the *de facto* rulers of the time. Many aspects of European culture had been quickly adopted by the Japanese and had already made a fairly deep impression upon the cultural life of the nation, but so severe were the persecutions of the new religion that soon almost all traces of the imported culture had disappeared. Even so, it proved all but impossible completely to purge the new European things from the Japanese mind. Here they had taken firm and deep root, and the influences upon the fine arts and even upon literature of these brief years of intercourse with the West were to prove very nearly impossible to erase. Soon Japan itself was producing objects full of new, European touches—visible in the design of clothing and textiles, in lacquer and ceramics, and in various kinds of painting. It was a veritable revolution in Japanese art.

The political revolution which was being carried out in Japan from about the middle of the sixteenth century on was in fact accomplishing its mission largely by the total and systematic destruction of all that was traditional. In the midst of the severe growing pains which naturally attended this process, in had come the guns and the religion of Western Europe, and, as we have seen, effective use had been made of both. But once Japan was finally unified and once the feudal structure of the Tokugawa regime firmly established, the reaction against the new things of Europe was to be as severe as earlier their reception had been eager. In their place the authorities were to look hopefully to Confucianism, the ancient system of thought and conduct developed in China, as a suitable moral and intellectual guide for their new society. Especially it was felt that the tenets of Confucianism with their emphasis upon loyalty and obedience were eminently suited to the dominant military classes of Japan's newly emerging feudal society.

The striking new art which developed in feudal Japan grew out of the social milieu whose growth we have been sketching above. It was an accurate reflection of the times in which it grew up, and hence like these times found its main points of departure in a vigorous denial of the past. The world of black and white, exemplified for example in the restrained, controlled Chinese-ink painting fancied by the Zen sect and its painter-priests, gave way before a gaudy new world of gold-leaf and bright lively color. Just as was the case in the Italian Renaissance, religious painting in Japan began to lose most of its religious significance, while painting in general more and more became something mainly employed to decorate and adorn the walls of the residences of the military class, not to mention the newly developed castles.

New themes were also quick to arise. The lower orders of society came to enjoy an increasingly lively way of life, and even a higher standard of living. Together with both went a new emphasis upon plebeian pleasures, upon outings and excursions, in addition to a new spirit of fun and gaiety in daily living. All these elements became, for the first time in Japanese art, the themes for painting. It was in a word genre painting, but the difference was that for the first time Japanese genre painting had moved into an important position in the area of the fine arts.

The first feudal castle to be built in Japan was, as we have seen, the Azuchi Castle of Nobunaga, erected in 1576. Nobunaga charged one of the most skilled painters of the period, Kano Eitoku, with the commission for the mural paintings which were to decorate its interior. Uufortunately the Azuchi Castle was later burned to the ground and none of its art survives, but contemporary literary evidence in the form of a passage from a work known as the *Nobunaga-ko Ki (The Records of Lord Nobunaga)* provides us with a description of the structure and its paintings.

The Azuchi Castle was a seven-story structure. The first and fifth floors were without paintings, but the others were decorated as follows:

Paintings in the "Flowers and Birds" tradition, including among their subject matter the flowering plum, pigeons, and pheasants, decorated the second floor. This motif was continued on the third floor, where it was supplemented by pictures of legendary Chinese figures such as Lü Tung-pin, a semihistorical Taoist and alchemist, and the fabulous "Queen Mother of the West" (Hsi-wang-mu). On the fourth floor the paintings showed trees among rocks, a contest between dragons and tigers, and legendary Chinese phoenixes among bamboos, pines, and paulownia trees, as well as the ancient Chinese models of virtuous reticence Hsü-yu and Ch'ao-fu. Finally, on the sixth floor were found, first of all, religious paintings, including the Buddha and his ten chief disciples, the Buddha preaching the Law, and improving scenes of various devils suffering in Buddhist hells, plus a variety of versions of the chief themes of traditional Chinese painting. Among these last were representations of the legendary "Three Emperors and Five Rulers" of ancient China, the ten chief disciples of Confucius, the "Four Recluses of Mt. Shang," the "Seven Sages of the Bamboo Grove," and the like.

What was the significance of these themes? The fourth floor was decorated, in other words, with paintings whose themes were familiar ones from the past. The Buddhist paintings of the sixth floor were of the type commonly kept in great reverence and even in secrecy in the temples of the time; here, in what was after all a military stronghold they were obviously employed primarily for their decorative qualities. Pictures showing the "Three Emperors and Five Rulers" of ancient China, and such subjects as the ten chief disciples of Confucius had been in the past favorite themes for the residences of nobles, while the "Four Recluses of Mt. Shang" and the "Seven Sages of the Bamboo Grove" were favorite themes among the Zen sect and its artistic adherents. In other words, the Azuchi Castle ended up being in effect a veritable "Comprehensive Collection of Oriental Art," embracing all schools and all tastes.

Of great importance is the note in the literary sources telling that all these pictures were "colored with gold." Traditionally, Japanese painting had almost never employed gold. For the first time in the paintings of Azuchi Castle the technique was apparently employed in which the entire surface to be painted was first filled with gold-leaf, the picture proper then being executed later on this gilded surface in heavy colors. It was a revolution in Japanese painting, and at the same time one of the most characteristic features of the period. It is no oversimplification to characterize the painting of early feudal Japan as an art of gold and colors, and the first important examples of this highly decorative technique appear to have been the paintings prepared for the Azuchi Castle by Kano Eitoku.

Hideyoshi in his turn also patronized Kano Eitoku and his decorative art. In 1583 Hideyoshi built Osaka Castle, parts of which are still standing today, and in 1585 the complex of palaces known as the Juraku-dai, or "Hostel of Assembled Pleasures." Both of these were adorned with paintings commissioned from Kano Eitoku. In 1587 he built his In-no-Gosho, and in 1590 this too was completed with paintings on the sliding panels which form the walls and separations between rooms in traditional Japanese architecture.

Today one can see preserved in various temples and other Buddhist institutions in the Kyoto area a great number of painted panels and wall-screens, many of which date from this very period. A considerable number of these are in fact attributed to the brush of Kano Eitoku. Most of these are supposed to have been brought to their present locations from such buildings as the Osaka Castle, the Juraku-dai, or the great castle erected at Fushimi, but among them there are of course many that it is most difficult to believe are actually the work of the great Kano Eitoku.

For one thing, there is the problem of their very number. However vigorous and productive an artist the famous Kano Eitoku may have been, it is difficult to conceive of him having turned out anything like this number of paintings by himself. Undoubtedly he had a great many disciples working in his school, and much of what survives today must be supposed to be their work rather than his. Probably, in the manner of European masters of earlier periods, Eitoku was often content to draw the cartoon or even simply the principal parts of the pictures, leaving his students to work together on following his design or completing the less interesting parts of the composition. In this sense many of the paintings are undoubtedly "joint works." At any rate, no panel painting bearing the signature of Eitoku is known to survive today.

As a matter of fact, almost all the panel paintings from this period to be seen in temples and similar buildings in the Kyoto area are unsigned, undoubtedly because so many of them are the product of the kind of "joint work" described above.

Most of these paintings to be seen at the present time resemble the literary accounts of

FIG. 5. Detail from "Genre Painting Screen" (Plate 19)
This representation of a tailor's shop is the oldest such painting known today and constitutes one of the forerunners of the popular "Views of Artisans" genre. See page 24, also caption to Plates 16–23.

the paintings in the Azuchi Castle in that they too are almost always executed in heavy colors on a gold-leaf ground. In subject matter they too concern legendary and traditional personalities from Chinese literature, in addition to birds, flowers, and various kinds of trees. Their scale is important, since in almost every case all subjects are rendered full-size, and with a liveliness which seems at times almost to propel them out of the picture toward the viewer. One great pine tree is often pictured alone, or with subsidiary rocks or flowers, towering up in full-scale majesty and filling the entire panel devoted to it. A vigorous and straightforward composition of this sort executed in colors on a gold-leaf ground fairly well sums up the panel painting of this particular period.

What was the significance for the time of this full-scale reality combined with the smash and exuberance of these expanses of gold leaf? First of all, the elements of ambitiousness in art of this kind must be remarked upon. For ambitious it is in the extreme to take hold of nature in this bold fashion, and to bring it in full size and full color right into the interiors of the period. Nor can we forget the uses to which these rooms thus decorated were put. Often for example they served as audience halls and ceremonial halls of state for the rulers for whom they were built. Here might well sit a local feudal lord or even the coming *de facto* ruler of Japan, resolutely squatting before the glittering and tremendously impressive background provided by panel paintings of this kind. Surely anyone received in audience by even a petty ruler amid such surroundings could hardly help being impressed with his power and supremacy. Hence there were social and political motives as well as artistic ones for this full-scale transplantation of nature into the halls and chambers of these early feudal structures.

As the era of Hideyoshi gave way to the seventeenth century, the art of the panel paintings gradually diminished in scale. Mighty pine trees of a size so great that formerly only one of their branches would have swept over a panel now appear in their entirety in reduced scale, while the limitless space of the older style gives way to the strictly defined limits of the panels themselves. Nature appears more and more in miniature, reduced to fit into the space available. The Japanese people at the time of Hideyoshi had been notably ambitious, their dreams taking them across the sea and into strange lands, but with his death they found their dreams shrinking and contracting, until at last they were reduced to locking themselves up into the self-imposed isolation of their "Closed Country." The plan and composition of the panel paintings exactly reflect these changes in the national outlook.

Panel painting in the period under discussion was largely in the hands of the painters of what came to be known as the Kano school, starting with Kano Eitoku, already mentioned, his son Mitsunobu, his adopted son Sanraku, and their various disciples and followers. The period was characterized, however, by the appearance of a host of remarkable painters who were not members of this dominant school, among whom Hasegawa Tohaku, Kaiho Yusho, and Soga Chokuan may be mentioned. Such men as these were soon engaged in a struggle with the members of the Kano school for leadership in the art world of the time. Each of the celebrated painters of the day, no matter what his school affiliations might have been, had under him often several hundred students and disciples to assist him in the execution of his commissions and other large orders. At this point in our consideration we must accordingly turn our attention from the celebrated masters of the traditional schools to their usually nameless assistants, for it was largely such unknown students and helpers who eventually found their real work in the production of genre paintings, thus giving artistic expression to the lives of the masses of Japanese society of the time.

IV. GENRE PAINTING

Japanese painting had, to be sure, long produced scenes of a genre nature, that is, scenes showing the daily lives of the people and their various customs. Often these were included in a type of formal painting known as *nenju-gyoji-e*, or "pictures of annual festivals," which recorded the ceremonies performed regularly each year at the imperial court both for their own interest and as a guide for the protocol of future celebrations. So it can hardly be said that genre painting as such was something that began afresh in the period here under consideration. At the same time, however, earlier genre painting had been of another nature, being concerned primarily with the upper classes and only accidentally touching upon the

FIG. 6. Detail from "Views in and around Kyoto" (Plate 28) by Kano Eitoku
The "Views of Artisans" genre developed out of scenes like this one showing Kyoto roofers at work.
The "Views in and around Kyoto" genre was, in fact, little more than a composite of artisan portraits.
See page 24, also caption to Plates 27 & 28.

life of the people. Its real purpose was far removed from the representation of genre scenes, however often these may have intruded their way in.

However, as we have already seen, it was just at this time that foreign trade became an important factor in Japanese life, and that both commercial activities and the life of the satellite communities around the castles began to flourish remarkably. The common people, who were most associated with these activities, also benefited most from them, and they soon found as a result that their economic position had very much changed for the better.

Here a contradiction arose. In Japan's newly forming feudal system the merchants and those following commercial occupations of any kind were by official definition to form the lowest level of society. No matter how important they might become economically they were to be absolutely forbidden to advance up in the social scale. Nor were they to have any voice at all in government. Hence their increasing social activities made possible by their increasing affluence were perforce restricted to the areas of general culture and amusements, except of course for commerce itself. There was very little else for them to do with the profits from their flourishing new businesses except to indulge in costly excursions, the Kabuki theater, and other basically unintellectual amusements. As one result the annual festivals which had long been held under the auspices of famous Buddhist temples and other religious institutions in Kyoto and elsewhere suddenly became extremely popular, as did group dances and dance spectacles in which a great number of persons could participate. All such events provided excuses to go on gay excursions and spend money with a minimum of intellectual preparation or social criticism.

Nor were festivals and dances all that were popular. The picnic too came into its own at about this time, with parties organized to go into the hills to view the flowering cherry in the spring, or the rich autumn foliage in the fall of the year, parties made even more lively by the lunches and the *saké* which they carried with them into the country. Along the banks and in the dry bed of the Kamo River in Kyoto side-show-like entertainment stalls presenting primitive versions of Kabuki performances sprung up one after the other. Here too freaks and jugglers could be viewed. Here the masses of the capital gathered and amused themselves until late into the night, for even those, and there were of course many, who remained poor as ever were feeling for the first time in their life something of a spirit of social liberation. In a sense the period was one which for the first time offered something of the delight and freedom of life to the major part of the population of the country, regardless of their social position.

For the plebeians of the period, this new joy of life was their first glimpse of their own existence as human beings. Hence it was that the lower orders of the people were to come onto the scene as a new force in art.

Partly this was because it was now simply impossible for the artists of the day completely to ignore the new, lively world that had grown up in the midst of Japanese society. In the earlier period when genre painting had been exclusively concerned with the formal duties and court protocol of the noble and military classes, such painting had been in a real sense a true reflection of the society of the time, for at the period these classes were the most important and vital ones in this society. But now the situation had changed fairly suddenly, and they found themselves replaced by the vigorous new lower classes. These were now the most vital segment of society, and hence their lively existence and folkways were bound to make their appearance in the art of the time.

As a result, a great many panel and folding-screen paintings were produced showing genre scenes from the lives of these newly important classes; their subject matter permits them to be classified into eight major groups, which will be treated here next in the order of their development.

1. Folding Screens Illustrated with Views in and around Kyoto.

These devoted themselves to the illustration of scenes in the city proper and the suburbs of the city of Kyoto, at the time the political and economic as well as the cultural heart of Japan. They are the first type to make its appearance.

2. Views Illustrating *Fêtes-Champêtres*.

The plebeians, now liberated to a certain extent socially and increasingly well-off economically are here shown revelling in their new-found liberty, enjoying themselves with picnic lunches and *saké* in field and on mountain, dancing, laughing, and in general making the most of their new status.

3. Views Illustrating Festivals and Ceremonies.

The regular festivals and public ceremonies of Shinto shrines and Buddhist temples were also favorites of the common people, who flocked to these colorful spectacles in great numbers. Their attendance of course made the festivals, many of them dating back to remote antiquity, even more lively and gaudy. Most spectacular of all was the celebration held in Kyoto at the Toyokuni Shrine in commemoration of the seventh anniversary of the death of Hideyoshi, a memorable event still recalled today. But even apart from special events such as this there were always plenty of regular festivals to attend. Among the most popular may be mentioned those of the Kamo Shrine in Kyoto, of the Yasaka Shrine in the Gion, Kyoto's pleasure quarter, and that of the ancient Hiyoshi Shrine in the hamlet of Otsu on the shores of Lake Biwa, a few hours from the capital. All of them were colorful celebrations held annually, and many paintings survive showing the people enjoying themselves at these events.

4. Views of Artisans.

No matter how important rural excursions and picnics might have been for the newly affluent masses or how interested they may have been in temple and shrine festivals, these are after all special events, and hardly something that happened every day. The artisan pictures were, on the contrary, concerned with everyday existence and in many cases with the very ways in which the common people made their living. Sets of such pictures were made showing twenty different varieties of artisans going about their business, including makers of Buddhist images, umbrella makers, writing-brush makers, armorers, and fan makers.

5. Views of the Kabuki Theater.

The Kabuki is of course Japan's characteristic popular theater form, said to have been begun about 1603. Many works survive showing the early stages of the art, then just in the process of its first development.

6. Views of Women.

These are scenes showing anywhere from five or six to thirty or forty women in various group activities.

7. Views of Individual Beauties.

These show, in isolated poses, celebrated individuals from among the then newly developing classes of licensed prostitutes, including dancers *(shirabyoshi),* bath women *(yuna),* and "ladies of pleasure" *(yujo).*

8. Folding Screens Showing the "Southern Barbarians."

This was a rather special type of subject matter, dealing with the various foreigners then becoming familiar to Japanese through foreign trade. ("Southern Barbarians" was a literary cliché adapted from Chinese and used as a general and not especially derogatory sobriquet for all foreigners at this period.) Hence works in this last category do not perhaps properly come under the head of genre painting in the strict sense.

The above eight general types are based on an analysis of the subject matter of early Japanese genre painting. As far as physical form is concerned a variety of types was used, including the folding screen *(byobu)*, the sliding panel *(fusuma)*, the vertical scroll *(kakemono)*, and the horizontal or hand scroll *(emaki)*. In decorative works intended for either castles or temples both sliding panels and the walls themselves were used for paintings. The folding screens were usually in six sections, and as the term implies, were so arranged that they could be folded up. The vertical scroll is the well-known hanging scroll used then as now for decorating the *toko-no-ma*, or alcove, the visual center of a Japanese room. The hand scroll is a long horizontal roll, a small portion of which is intended to be viewed at one time as the whole is slowly unrolled from one hand and at the same time rolled up in the other. Thus the painting of the time employed a great variety of spatial types, ranging from the almost full-scale sliding panels and folding screens down to the comparatively small-scale hanging and hand scrolls.

Even within a single type there was a considerable amount of variation in size. Some folding screens have six sections, some eight, others only two. Certain large ones measure 1.80 meters high by 4 meters long, some medium-size ones are 1 meter high and 3 meters long, while the smaller ones are 0.80 meters by 2 meters. Screens of these greatly varying sizes were necessary because of the large variety of uses to which they were put in rooms of various types. The largest ones usually found employment in the audience halls of feudal lords and nobility, while the smallest were suitable for the less pretentious rooms of the common people.

Even though many of the pictures coming under the classifications above drew their subject matter from the lives and activities of the common people, this is not to imply that all of them were made to order for or commissioned by such persons. In fact, it is thought that in the first stages of the art nearly all of them were commissioned by feudal lords and other members of the warrior class. Even though their economic position had greatly improved, the common people were in the first stages of the art still far from the taste necessary to appreciate it fully. Gradually, from about 1600 on this situation changed, however, and with the development of the necessary taste naturally came the desire on the part of the common people to beautify their lives as much as possible. With this development the true popularization of genre painting itself was all but completed.

From this point on we find ample evidence for this popularization in the form of small- and medium-size folding screens, ideally suited to the mode of living of the lower classes. Other evidence is available in the fact that from this point on pictures dealing with the same theme are found reproduced over and over, eventually even leading to the stocking of ready-made pictures.

It must be emphasized that Japan's early genre painting was not something which developed overnight; rather it was in large measure the result of adaptations of earlier styles of long standing and tradition. For example, in the case of the first and earliest class of subject matter listed above, the folding screens illustrated with views in and around Kyoto, it is easy to identify their origins in traditional painting going back to the Heian period (794–1185) and the years immediately following, when views of celebrated scenic spots in and near the capital were often prepared for the nobles, whom they served partly as guidebooks and partly as sources of topographical information. None of these survive, but we may assume that they dealt with the scenery of famous places and also with genre scenes centering about them. Also, it is clear that the earlier works in this tradition were rather different in general approach from the ones we are discussing here. The earlier ones appear to have been relatively formal, abstract treatments of their subjects, in contrast to the realistic concern with the actualities of scenery which we find in the later genre works.

An example which may be cited of the latter is the folding screen "Views in and around Kyoto" in the Machida Collection (Plates 25 & 26). Here the residences of the shogun and other important civil and military officials are reproduced with such fidelity that it is pos-

FIG. 7. Detail from "The River Bed at Shijo" (Plate 66)
The cold objectivity of the earlier genre paintings that tended to "look down" on the plebeian subject matter they portrayed was replaced by the warmer, more subjective approach of later works such as this. See page 24, also caption to Plate 4.

sible with complete certainty to assign this work to the period 1521–28 simply on this basis alone. Again, in the folding screen "Views in and around Kyoto" by Kano Eitoku in the Uesugi Collection (Plates 27 & 28) we find the streets of the capital shown as they were before Hideyoshi introduced certain far-reaching changes in the course of redesigning the ancient city; hence the screen can without hesitation be assigned to the period before these changes, which were carried out during the period 1573–92. Thus in the genre painting here being considered it is often quite possible, so faithful are the artists to the subjects they are depicting and so literal is their approach, to date works simply by the buildings and city streets appearing in them! This is certainly adequate evidence that the early genre art had succeeded in breaking away from the traditional formality and abstraction of Japanese painting.

It is this fidelity to life which especially distinguishes most of these genre scenes from earlier paintings dealing with famous scenic spots. Under category 2 above the earliest known example is the folding screen "Autumn-Foliage Viewing at Takao" (Plate 24). This shows a group of plebeians engaged in viewing the brilliant autumn foliage at a place in Kyoto called Takao, and is remarkable for its genuine genre touches. Today only this one screen with its autumn scene is known, but it is most likely that originally it formed one of a pair, the other being devoted to a similar spring scene. It is also possible, since in the upper-left-hand corner of the present screen a snow-covered mountain can be seen, that what we have here is rather part of a series covering the four seasons, and that there may have been in addition representations of spring and summer in some form or other. Hence it would appear that the screen might originally have been part of a traditional set of "Four Seasons" pieces.

Traditional Japanese painting, like that of the Chinese, often divided its subject matter into seasonal groups, producing sets of pictures treating the same or roughly the same theme at different times of the year. Natural scenery was of course most often treated in this fashion, with one picture for spring, one for summer, one for fall, and one for winter, and views of birds and flowers were also often divided into a series of similar treatments. Thus if the Takao screen is indeed part of some such series, it shows a continuation of the old traditional division of themes over the seasons, but with the important replacement of the traditional birds and flowers by the lively human subjects.

The fourth category above also has traditional origins, which are to be found in the type of picture called "Artisans' Song Contests" *(shokunin uta-awase-e)*, popular from the Muromachi period (1333–1573) on. The genre treatments of this subject matter did not simply take over the earlier formal tradition; they of course expanded and developed it. But even so, these genre representations of artisans could hardly have come into being without a full consciousness of the earlier tradition.

Thus, the coming into full flower of genre art in Japan was hardly either a sudden or a precipitate development. Behind it lies the full formal tradition of earlier periods, in which tradition the new developments were sturdily rooted. What is most important is clearly to distinguish the ways in which the new here differed from the old; mainly, it was in the approach of the new artists toward their subject matter. Leaving the tradition and where necessary consciously isolating their work from it, they went ahead with a new realistic attitude, putting the focus of their attention upon the colorful, lively activities of the common people. Their forms were often traditional ones, but their subject matter was new, and their realistic approach to it soon came to be the dominant factor in the art of the time.

The currents of the new genre tradition begin to change markedly about 1600. An important landmark in the development of the art at this point is the folding screen "Festival Ceremonies at the Toyokuni Shrine," (Plates 39 & 40) thought to have been executed in 1606. Hideyoshi had died in 1598. Six years later in 1604 a special extraordinary series of rituals and ceremonies were held in his memory at the Toyokuni Shrine in Kyoto. Literary sources of the period tell us something of what went on at the time; the festivities, which began on the fourteenth day of the eighth month of the lunar calendar and lasted for several days, seem literally to have been conducted on a scale hitherto unknown in Japan. Ceremonial dances based on rice-planting rituals *(dengaku)* as well as traditional, formal comic dances *(sarugaku)* were performed as part of the worship service before the shrine buildings, in the presence of a large assembly of Shinto priests and warriors all sitting rigidly at a formal position of attention.

Another special dance prepared for the occasion, the "Toyokuni Dance," was performed by over five hundred citizens of Kyoto in front of the Great Buddha Image Hall of the Hoko-ji while more than a thousand spectators thronged the grounds in what contemporary sources mention as a scene of "indescribable confusion." This particular folding screen is said to have been painted by the artist Kano Naizen on the basis of his personal observations of the event, completed two years later, and presented to the shrine as an act of piety.

In addition to the folding screen dealing with this scene from the brush of Kano Naizen (Plates 39 & 40), another similar work (Plates 37 & 38) is also known, but this is the product of some nameless popular artist specializing in genre works, and far different from the work of the tradition-conscious painters of the Kano school. Its composition is almost the same as that of the Kano version, but in its treatment of the lively confusion and of the action of the figures it is far more vigorous. Hence it would appear to be quite in order to suppose that as early as 1604 there was in existence a group of specialized artists who dealt in genre scenes of this type and who were already well apart from the Kano school traditions, and that even this early their work had achieved considerable stature.

The existence of these two versions is important for various other reasons. For one thing, it shows that a fairly long period of development had gone before in order to make possible the sheer draftsmanship necessary for such true-to-life representations of the human figure. The artists were concerned with transmitting as much of the bustle and confusion of the lively scene as possible to posterity; hence their precise attention to small as well as to large details, and the objective, narrative approach which they adopted. They were reporters "covering" the event for posterity, as it were, and this quality of accurate, factual "reportage" came to be one of the basic characteristics of the genre style in Japan.

The screen showing the celebrations at the Toyokuni Shrine was undoubtedly painted on commission from some feudal lord. Literary sources tell us that the screen by Kano Naizen was done to the order of Katagiri Ichimasa, but the other example now in the collection of the Tokugawa Remei-kai was also probably made to order for some member of the military class. Once again we are reminded of the important fact the even though it was the common people who formed the main theme of the genre paintings, such paintings were not primarily appreciated by their subjects, at least in the first stages of the art.

Rather, the artists who in this fashion worked out these large-scale narrative presentations of living scenes, and the objective techniques which made their reproduction on large surfaces possible, were generally "looking down" upon their subjects. The term expresses perfectly the perspective they employed, as well as their sociological orientation. Naturally, so long as this "looking down" continued the genre art which it produced could hardly be appreciated by those whom it pictured. It was basically the feudal lords, for example, who were interested in series of pictures showing workmen and artisans going about their everyday, but to the upper-classes "quaint," tasks. They were the ones most interested in learning how carvers of Buddhist images, for example, went about their business, not the carvers themselves who knew it only too well.

The views of scenes "In and around Kyoto," a well-established type, were really little more than comprehensive groups of artisan portraits; blow up any tiny section of one of the former and you have one of the latter. The earlier *uta-awase-e* tradition was left well behind here, in favor of the new. The artisan pictures came eventually to stand on their own as an established type, but their expression remained cold and objective. They were scenes viewed from the top, looking down.

In time this too changed, and the cold objectivity of the early examples comes to be replaced with a far warmer, more subjective approach. One of the best examples of the transition steps necessary for this process is the folding screen "The River Bed at Shijo," (Plates 4, 66 & 67) whose main theme is the early Kabuki-like entertainments staged in the dry bed and along the banks of Kyoto's chief river at the point where it intersects Shijo, "Fourth Avenue."

It is important to note that today at least four different versions of this screen are known. Two of them are medium-sized ones, each of two sections, while the other two are extremely small, almost miniature examples, each of six sections. In the case of the works dealing with scenes in and around Kyoto discussed above, the well-known specimens are all large-scale pieces, but many others are also known to exist today, all of medium or small size. This shift from large-size pieces to smaller and smaller ones, especially in the case of the folding screens, no doubt indicates the gradual shift from decorative works designed for large apartments and halls in great mansions to more modest ones for more limited structures. That we find smaller and smaller examples of such topics as the "Scenes in and around Kyoto" and the Shijo scene can only mean that gradually these paintings were being more and more appreciated and employed for decoration by the lower orders of the population.

FIG. 8. Detail from "The River Bed at Shijo" (Plate 70)
The narrative, documentary character of the genre works makes them invaluable as social and cultural records of the time. This detail showing an early sumo *match is one of the earliest of its kind.*

Another thing of interest in the Shijo screen is that all the figures in it were almost certainly executed by unknown painters. Relatively few early Japanese genre paintings are by recognized painters, at any rate; about the only ones that can be cited are the folding screen "Autumn-Foliage Viewing at Takao" by Kano Hideyori (Plate 24); the folding screen "Views in and around Kyoto" by Kano Eitoku (Plates 27 & 28); the folding screen "Festival Ceremonies at the Toyokuni Shrine" by Kano Naizen (Plates 39 & 40); and the folding screen "Pleasures under the Blossoms" by Kano Naganobu (Plate 53).

All these were recognized artists of the time, with their own proper places in the tradition, but the rest of the screens and paintings of this type are all by unknowns. Sometimes paintings that are unsigned can still be assigned to the style of a particular school; thus the folding screen "Flower-Viewing at Daigo" (not shown in the present volume) is in the style of the Hasegawa school; the folding screen of "Flower-Viewing and Falconry" (Plates 50, 51 & 52) in the style of the Unkoku school; the murals of the Nagoya Castle in the style of the Kano school, etc.

But others can be assigned to no particular traditional style. These include for example the Tokugawa Reimei-kai version of the Toyokuni Shrine screen, and the Shijo screen now under discussion. Here the painting is neither Kano school nor Tosa school nor any of the others, but in a distinctive new style. What does this signify? For one thing, it points to certain important changes among the artists of the time, and to certain alterations in their methods of making a living.

The great castles and noble residences of the time, like those at Azuchi, Fushimi, and Osaka, were literally filled with decorative paintings, all usually done on gold ground. These were usually simply commissioned in job lots from famous painters such as Eitoku, Mitsunobu, or Sanraku. In most cases the whole project had to be completed within a very short period of time, often in only a few months. Of course such projects could not possibly be executed by any one man, much less by the few famous painters from whom they were usually commissioned. Rather they were, as we have seen, in large part executed by the crowds of students and disciples whom each celebrated artist had in his studio.

These large numbers of assistants found themselves in serious economic difficulties when the times changed and the great castles and palatial residences which had once called for their skills became rarer and rarer. Their place was gradually taken by smaller residences, while at the same time the scale of painting employed to decorate them correspondingly diminished. Most such artists were, to put it simply, soon out of work, for the mass orders which had once kept them busy no longer came to their masters. These are the suddenly unemployed artists who became the *machi-eshi*, the anonymous painter artisans of the towns, producing works to commission if commissions were forthcoming and if not keeping themselves busy by turning out a stock of ready-made pictures for future sale.

Naturally their first field of concentration was genre painting showing townsmen in their daily activities. Soon they enjoyed a virtual monopoly not only on these but also on the production of paintings showing scenes in and around Kyoto—always good sellers to persons anxious to take back some souvenir of the big city!—and on the production of paintings showing various aspects of foreign trade—the "Southern Barbarians" theme—which was just at the moment the center of popular attention. Today we often have ten or even twenty surviving examples of the same picture, eloquent testimony to the industry and enthusiasm with which these anonymous artists went about their trade.

But for them to ply their new trade, it was first necessary that they develop a new style—a style suited to the lively, realistic presentations they were seeking. Most of them had been trained under masters of the Kano school; but the strong, dramatic line of this type of painting, well suited as it was to the classical themes of Chinese antiquity, was manifestly unsuitable when faced, for example, with the problem of depicting the supple, elegant charm of a Japanese dancer from some lively city's gay quarter. A newer, softer, more emotional line was necessary for them if they were to have any success at all with their new themes.

We can see good examples of this new, vivid expressive technique in the figures of the dancing women in the Seika-do Shijo screen, or in the same work in the comic figure of the attendant at the entrance to the small hut. It goes without saying that the perfection of this new technique, the technique of the nameless journeymen painters of the towns, was an essential step in the development of Japanese genre painting.

Through roughly the center of the city of Kyoto there flows even today the Kamo River, in time of rain often a dangerous and troublesome stream, but for most of the year a mere trickle of tepid water with broad, inviting dry beds of sand and gravel on either side. In the open spaces presented by these river beds it was the custom, since remote antiquity, to stage variety shows and entertainments, often of a rather rowdy character, for the poorer people of the capital. The dry bed of the Kamo River has hence long been a kind of midway for the ancient capital—a combination of Coney Island and Atlantic City Boardwalk, to choose perhaps wildly inappropriate parallels. Here it was that in 1603 according to a widely accepted tradition a renegade Shinto priestess named Okuni first put on her dances called Kabuki—from an archaic verb meaning literally "to cavort or fool about"—causing a sensation with her novel movements and striking costumes. Kabuki, the people's theater of feudal Japan, came to life in such cirumstances as these.

Imitations were of course quick to appear. In the section of Kyoto called Rokujo, named after the Six Main Avenue of the old imperial city plan and celebrated in literature as the residence of the "Lady of the Sixth Ward" in *The Tale of Genji*, performances imitating those of Okuni were soon being offered. Their performers were prostitutes; their acts consisted of various dances to the rhythms of the *shamisen*, a three-stringed musical instrument then but newly imported to Japan *via* the Ryukyus. The original profession of the actresses, however, was by far their greatest attraction, with the result that such theatrical entertainments never attained more than the status of animated advertisements for their more ordinary accomplishments, and the government took official notice of the situation by prohibiting the entire thing in 1629. Their place was taken by similar troupes of attractive young men, who survive in today's Kabuki in the form of the female impersonators, a remnant of this early prohibition of stage performances by women. Even today the true Kabuki stage of Japan employs only male actors for all its roles.

The Seika-do Shijo screen has as its central theme a view of the Kabuki entertainments before the prohibition of appearances by women, and offers in addition a panoramic glimpse of all the diversions once available in the dry bed of the Kamo River. Internal evidence points to around 1615 as its date. Its content is thoroughly popular and entertainment-centered, but the line and composition which give it expression are admirably suited to such a theme. Like the Toyokuni Shrine screen and the other views of festivals mentioned above, the Seika-do Shijo screen is an extremely important one since the near certainty with which it can be dated provides an invaluable bench mark in the study of the development of Japanese painting.

From about 1620 on we find the art gradually beginning to lose much of its talent for presenting documentary records of places, people, and events. In their place we find more and more the everyday commonplaces of the lives of the townsmen. Examples of this tendency which can be cited are the folding screen "Women" in the collection of the Yamato Bunka-kan (not shown in the present volume), and "The Hikone Screen" in the Ito Collection (Plates 1 & 88).

The folding screen "Women" is a large work in six sections showing eighteen women in close to life-size, beautifully dressed and reflecting the change toward elegance which increasing prosperity was bringing into the dress of the townsmen. In its time, this screen was undoubtedly something of a fashion plate showing the newest modes.

"The Hikone Screen" shows fifteen variously dressed men and women in interior and exterior settings, but there is little overt indication of interior and exterior. The section which is intended to be the interior shows a landscape screen among the room's furnishings, and also the figures appearing here are seated, while those in the exterior portion are standing. But nothing else is indicated of place, because the intention is simply to display the decadent, gaudy beauty of the figures shown.

Another important example which can be cited here is the celebrated "Bath Women" (Plate 8) now in the collection of the Atami Museum of Fine Art. Bath women *(yuna)* were a variety of rather low-class public prostitutes employed in the public bathing establishments of Kyoto and Edo (Tokyo) from about the beginning of the seventeenth century. The painting shows six of them taking a stroll down the street, but it intended to show but little of their sordid way of life. Rather the artist has concentrated, and with great success, on their decadent charm, and it is his masterful depiction of this which gives the picture its great interest.

The three works just discussed have several things in common. They all deal with subjects which were commonly seen parts of daily life in the towns of the period. They all focus on particular aspects of this life, namely the beauty of costumes and the charm of the human figure for their dramatic and artistic effect. All of the documentary qualities of the Toyokuni Shrine screen, for example, are by this time lost, and interest has shifted in a spectacular fashion to the individuals who comprised the crowded scenes in which the earlier works delighted.

This is the reason we find around this period that the number of figures in individual works declines, and that there are few if any compositions showing large crowds. As the point of view and the interests of the viewers changed so too did the composition, and with the composition, the subject matter. These tendencies are particularly noticeable from about 1650 on, and develop into what comes to be known as the style of the "Kambun beauty," a general term used to designate pictures showing a single, standing beauty. The term derives from the name of the reign period from 1661 to 1672, the Kambun period, during which the largest number of these pieces was turned out.

Poses were also varied. Sometimes the left hand is hidden within the sleeve, while the right grasps the front part of the skirt of the outer garment and holds it together and slightly up; sometimes the left is shown holding out the sleeve while the right holds a dancing fan, with one foot lifted in a dance step. Almost all examples known to survive today show similar poses, a tribute to the amount of formalization which this type of painting soon achieved, while at the same time testifying to the near mass-production methods by which they were turned out.

These pictures of beauties stress of course the charm of the human form both at rest and in movement, but there is little or nothing here of the accurate recording of the various aspects of daily human life. Documentary and reportage qualities are lost, giving place to a delight in the beauty of the individual which is to become the hallmark of Japanese painting.

From this point on, the story would take us off into the development of the *ukiyo-e*, and notably into a consideration of Japan's colored woodblock prints; to follow this up in detail would take us far afield from our immediate subject. Still we may point out that the *ukiyo-e* pictures take as their point of departure the paintings of beauties here introduced.

These pictures of beauties were actual paintings, mounted in the form of vertical, hanging scrolls *(kakemono)*. They were of course not prints. This type of art was suitable as long as powerful (and by the same token rich) feudal lords were its patrons, but when it came to depend upon the common people for its patronage, things had to change. A kind of art was demanded which permitted near mass production of identical pictures, which could then be sold for a few coppers apiece. These requirements could only be met by the development of woodblock printing. Soon the genre artist was not producing finished paintings any more but only the basic underpainting to be used for carving the woodblocks that would, when printed in sequence, produce the actual works of art, the dazzling, multi-colored *ukiyo-e* prints.

Japan's Renaissance period, then, if we are to admit that she has indeed had one, begins about the middle of the sixteenth century. Mention has already been made of the role played in the triggering of this Renaissance by the advances of Portuguese traders into the Far East, and by the examples of European culture which they brought with them. Today there are some forty surviving paintings showing the "Southern Barbarians," eloquent testimony to the tremendously seminal effect of these early contacts between Japan and the rest of the world. Both the new religion of these foreigners and the material advances which accompanied it were to leave important traces in Japanese cultural life, eventually even leading to overseas adventures involving Japanese. It was an age of a vigorous, virile national spirit in these islands, and as such wonderfully well caught and reflected by the heroic, large-scale paintings which decorated feudal castles and mansions throughout the land. With the foreign contacts came enhanced economic possibilities for thousands of persons until then dismissed as beneath social notice; and with their new economic life came also new interests in the outdoors, in sightseeing, and in excursions. Every level and stratum of Japanese society was alive, on the move, and vigorous.

Art, too, was part and parcel of the whole age; like Japanese society, it too was vital, energetic, and constantly changing.

But soon—too soon, in fact—all this was to come to an end. Tokugawa Ieyasu, the new unifier of Japan, built his feudal stronghold in Edo and with this act instituted a rigid feudal system which was to survive unchallenged for the next three hundred years. Sooner than anyone realized, the freedom and brilliance of the sixteenth century had been expelled from Japanese society, and Japan was once again an isolated island kingdom in cultural as well as in geographical fact. The pine and the flowering plum, once painted so vigorously that they seemed about to leave the frame of the composition, shrunk and shrunk till they became, in the art of the feudal era, almost mere details in the over-all composition. Gone too are the crowds of revelling dancers, and silent are their musicians. All that is left, finally, are the decadent beauties of the *ukiyo-e* prints.

Plates

2. GENRE PAINTING SCREEN (detail)

Coll. Tokyo National Museum
Colors on paper. Eight-fold screen; each panel 67.27×41.81 cm.
Entire screen shown in Plates 16–23.

Shown here is a section of an eight-fold screen; the entire work is devoted to annual observances and celebrations, and the section reproduced here shows a group of people carrying a noon lunch into the fields where it will be eaten by the farmers busy with the spring replanting of the rice paddies. During the busy rice planting season in Japan it is customary to eat the noon meal in the fields, to save the precious minutes that would otherwise be lost in going back to the farmhouses.

Here an elderly man leads the procession of the food bearers; across his shoulders is hung the traditional arrangement of a stout pole from which hang wooden containers for soup and vegetables. The women who follow him carry large wooden tubs full of rice and other food, as the whole procession carefully picks its way along the narrow pathway between the flooded paddy fields.

An air of happy interest in the work of the peasants pervades the composition, in a way that makes the present example quite rare in the field of Japanese genre painting. The artist obviously was well acquainted with the life of the people living on the land, and was able to bring much sympathy and interest to his depiction of their daily work. It is in this type of painting, with its easy familiarity with the activities and interests of the lower orders of society, that Japan's lively art of the sixteenth and seventeenth centuries really begins to come into its own.

Pictures of annual observances and events were popular in Japan as early as the eleventh or twelfth century, and were used for decorating folding screens and sliding wall panels, as well as in illustrations for long scrolls. Most of them, however, were devoted to scenes centering about the imperial court or the activities of noble families, and showed little concern in the doings of the common people.

Most of these early examples of the genre are now lost, and we know of their contents only through literary references, but from these it is clear that they sometimes included the annual spring replanting of the rice paddies and the autumn rice harvest among their traditional lists of annual events to be commemorated. It is, of course, virtually impossible to guess how these early examples treated, for example, scenes of rice planting, but it is probably safe to assume that their treatment had little if anything in common with the easy, plebeian style of the late-sixteenth-century work of which a detail is reproduced here.

In this detail from a folding screen, four young men and women are enjoying themselves in the performance of a dance; one strikes a small drum held in the hand, while the other three hold fans. The detail is the section of the screen with the most striking movement of any; partly, the artist has here achieved this lively effect by his attention to the costumes, especially to the long, trailing ends of the headdresses which the dancing figures are wearing. As may be seen in the reproduction of the entire screen the four figures are shown dancing in the garden before an octagonal Buddhist temple building.

Among similar genre representations of dancing figures the present one is somewhat unusual in that it shows persons of the upper classes. Outdoor dancing of the kind pictured here was popular among the lower classes during the period from which much of the painting reproduced in the present volume dates, but the screen reproduced is interesting evidence that it also enjoyed considerable vogue among the upper classes.

4. THE RIVER BED AT SHIJO (detail from left screen of a pair)

Important Cultural Property. Coll. Seika-do
Colors on paper. Pair of two-fold screens; each screen 164.3×172.0 cm.
Entire screens shown in Plates 66 & 67

Reproduced is a small section from a screen showing a great variety of scenes taking place in the area which may properly be considered the birthplace of Japan's Kabuki theater —the dry river bed of the Kamo River, at its crossing with Shijo Avenue, in Kyoto.

Here in this popular amusement quarter for the plebeians of the ancient imperial capital were available primitive Kabuki performances, marionette theaters, and every other imaginable kind of attraction, all busy enticing avid customers into the shops, huts, stalls, and theaters erected on the inviting stretches of level river bank.

Chief among all these attractions was of course the then newly invented Kabuki skits and dances, said to have been begun in 1603 by a certain Okuni, traditionally a renegade Shinto priestess from the famous Grand Shrines of Izumo. Here she applied what she remembered of the fundamentals of ritual singing and dancing to the development of a much more lively and far more remunerative type of performance. Soon Kyoto was full of Kabuki theaters, their casts largely drawn from the harlot population of the capital's many segregated quarters of commercialized vice.

The detail reproduced shows several such early Kabuki actresses performing a circular dance on stage, while in the center the eye is caught by the arresting figure of another actress sitting on a tigerskin-covered chair playing on the three-stringed *shamisen*.

The *shamisen*, today the most commonly used musical instrument in the Japanese theater, was originally imported into Japan from the Ryukyus; even its name is thought not to be original in Japan, but to be a Japanese corruption of a Ryukyu original referring to the fact that its sound box was originally covered with snakeskin. (Today cat or dog hide is usually used.)

When the Kabuki in Japan was just beginning to develop the *shamisen* was still a newly introduced musical instrument, and extremely popular because of its sheer novelty. Even in this tiny detail of the much larger original, the artist has been more than successful in introducing something of a feeling of decadent charm into the figures of his lively dancing actresses.

5. *THE PLEASURES OF WOMEN* (detail)

Important Art Object. Coll. Yahata Yotaro
Colors on paper. Four-fold screen; 86.2×219.2 cm.
Entire screen shown in Plate 89

The two panels reproduced are the two left-hand ones of a four-fold screen, and show a lively group of women amusing themselves outdoors. They loll about voluptuously on a red carpet spread over the lawn as they enjoy a pipeful of tobacoo, drink, play the *shamisen*, and gossip.

The other sections of the screen show similar scenes, and the only male figure to be found is the solitary standing one in the right of the present detail. Probably the whole was intended to show a group of bath women whom he has taken on a gay trip into the country to amuse him and themselves.

The bath women of the period were employees of public bathing establishments, where they were supposed to provide personal attentions for the customers. Ability to sing and dance were important accomplishments for them, however, and in fact they formed the lowest class among the many varieties of prostitutes who prospered in Japan's early cities. Their lot was hardly a very happy one, and here the artist has surely been more than usually successful in indicating, in their very facial expressions, much of their trying way of life. Even their crude, heavy make-up has here been faithfully caught.

6. *HONDA HEIHACHIRO PORTRAIT SCREEN* (detail)
Important Cultural Property. Coll. Reimei-kai
Colors on paper, gold ground. Two-fold screen; each panel, 72.72×78.78 cm.
Entire screen shown in Plate 96

The detail reproduced is from the right portion of the screen reproduced in its entirety in Plate 96, and is traditionally believed to show Sen-hime, "Princess Sen," and her lover Honda Heihachiro. The princess was married in 1607 when she was only eleven to Hideyori, the son of the military leader Toyotomi Hideyoshi. When Hideyoshi's stronghold, the Osaka Castle, fell before the forces of Tokugawa Ieyasu, the Tokugawa leader himself gave orders to one of his followers, Sakasaki Dewa-no-Kami Masatomo, to rescue the young girl from the scene of destruction; according to some this concern was due to the fact that the princess was a granddaughter of Ieyasu.

Masatomo rescued the princess on condition that she should consent to marry him, but once safely out she refused, finding the terrifying warrior's countenance of her rescuer repulsive in the extreme. Later she became first the lover and then the wife of a handsome youth named Honda Heihachiro. Heihachiro soon died, however, and his death was widely thought to have been caused by the hatred which Masatomo bore to him. (The belief that being bitterly hated may well cause a person's death is an old one in Japan.)

The story, at any rate, is still well known, and it is thought that the detail illustrated is meant to show its chief characters. The identification is somewhat verified by the fact that the plump female figure in the center of the detail wears a kimono with the hollyhock crest of the Tokugawa house, and also by the fact that a textile with the same hollyhock crest design has been used to bind the edges of the screen. In feudal times the use of this crest was rigidly reserved for the Tokugawa house.

The figures shown with her here are notable for their voluptuous charm, which approaches a hint of illicit pleasures. In the left section of the screen the figure of a man about to be handed a letter by a maidservant is thought to be that of Honda Heihachiro (see Plate 96).

7. *DANCING FIGURES* (detail)

Important Art Object. Coll. City of Kyoto
Colors on paper, gold ground. Six-fold screen; 63.2×245.8 cm.
Entire screen shown in Plate 90

The detail shows a single dancing figure from among six mounted on a small six-fold screen. Originally, it is thought, these formed part of a set of two six-fold screens, showing a total of twelve dancing figures. The remaining ones can today be identified as including the "Dancing Figure" in the collection of Mr. Umehara Ryuzaburo (see Plate 91), and the four-fold screen in the Higuchi Collection (not shown in the present volume); thus only one of the original twelve figures is still unaccounted for.

The young dancers are colorfully garbed, and each holds a fan daintily in her hand as she goes through the motions of her dance. Each pose is different, for the artist has gone directly to life for his models and has succeeded in bringing the true beauty of the living dance into his work.

Whether the dancers here meant to be performers in the early "women's" Kabuki or simply ordinary prostitutes is not clear, nor is the identity of the artist known. From the style with which the waterfowl to be seen on the fan are painted, however, it is possible to conjecture that the work is the product of someone working in the traditions of the Kano school. Whoever he was, he surely must be admitted to have excelled in his self-chosen speciality of painting beauties of the time.

The dancers' colorful garments make much use of the familiar "tie-dye" pattern which was in vogue at the period, so it would probably not be far from the mark to assume that the painter was probably just as interested in showing examples of modish clothing and fashion as he was in portraying interesting female models. In fact, much of the genre painting of the time was fully as interested in recording fashions in dress as in dealing with any of its other themes.

8. BATH WOMEN

Important Cultural Property. Coll. Atami Museum of Fine Art
Colors on paper. Single panel; 72.6×80.3 cm.

Bath women *(yuna)* were employees of public bathing establishments in Edo and Kyoto, and began to be popular from about the beginning of the seventeenth century on. During the daylight hours their duties were limited to helping around the bath houses, and to such simple tasks as rinsing off the customers' backs, but with the coming of evening they spread their rush mats in the bathing establishments and began to serve drinks and food, entertaining their customers with singing and dancing. The natural result was that in no time the term "bath woman" came simply to be a rather transparent euphemism for harlot. So popular did the institution prove that the government took steps to forbid it entirely in 1657.

The celebrated genre painting reproduced here shows a group of such women on a stroll through the streets during the daytime, and surely it is unnecessary to call attention to the tremendous talent and skill with which the artist has captured their thoroughly coarse and crude but also completely lively and uninhibited manner.

Identification of the figures as "bath women" is assured by the kimono worn by the second from the left; it bears a stylized decorative device of a Chinese character to be understood as meaning "bath." The composition is especially notable for its life and movement; partly this has been achieved by pairing off the six figures into three groups of two each, and posing each group independently of the others, yet still balancing them. The liveliness and action of the resulting effect were qualities all but unknown to the older, traditional styles of Japanese painting.

The figures are in motion literally down to the tips of their toes, and not the least of the notable points of the work is the remarkable amount of energy the artist has packed into his depiction of their busy, prancing feet. That the identity of the master responsible for this screen is unknown is a great pity, for he was surely one of the most talented persons to work in the field of Japanese genre painting.

9. THE "NUN"

Coll. Atami Museum of Fine Art
Colors on paper. Single panel; 62.12×25.57 cm.

For a time in the early sixteenth century there was a certain vogue for wandering prostitutes who enticed their customers by dressing in the traditional habits of Buddhist nuns
and strolling about the city streets, often attracting further attention by chanting mildly
suggestive poems. The detail illustrated is said to picture one of these women, though here
she has by and large abandoned the austerity of a nun's habit for more colorful garments.
Still, there remains about her something of the mock piety with which these harlots are
supposed to have made themselves popular.

Here all that remain of the inky black tones of a proper nun's habit are her black girdle
and the hint of black undergarments which she allows to peep out at her neckline and hem;
but these if anything only throw into even sharper contrast the brilliant gold of her outer
garment. Probably the box she carries in her hand contains the poems she will chant.

If any doubt remained about her profession, however, the sight of her frankly suggestive
eyes peering out from under her basket-like hat would remove all hesitation.

10. KAIGETSU-DO ANDO: COURTESAN
Coll. Takeuchi Kimpei
Colors on paper. Single panel; 119.29×48.48 cm.

This is the celebrated "Kaigetsu-do beauty," half turned away from the viewer and arching her long figure across the entire panel, to present to the eye a fascinating vista filled with her unbelievably ornate kimono. Further heightening the bold impression of her pose are the thick, determined lines with which the figure is outlined.

Today over a hundred similar paintings are known to exist, and almost all of them employ the same composition. This type of figure is generally known as the "Kaigetsu-do beauty," a term derived from the studio name (Kaigetsu-do) of a certain Ando, who is revered as the founder of a school of figure painting which for about thirty years from 1700 on was extremely popular in Japanese genre painting.

The Kaigetsu-do painters maintained their headquarters in Suwa-cho of the Asakusa district in Edo, where they were conveniently located for selling their pictures to patrons returning home from a night amid the pleasures of the nearby Yoshiwara. In fact, their art was very nearly limited to the mass production of what were in effect publicity pictures for the inmates of Edo's largest quarter of commercialized vice. No doubt the demands and limitations imposed upon them by the necessity of mass production account for the fact that almost all of their work known today is limited to this same striking pose.

Ando himself was involved as the go-between in the notorious affair of 1714 in which Ejima, a lady-in-waiting at the Tokugawa court, was convicted of carrying on an affair with the popular Kabuki actor Ikushima Shingoro, and for his pains was banished to Miyake Island. In the feudal social system of the time there could hardly have been a more disgraceful crime than to have arranged this illicit liaison between a woman close to the shogun's family and an actor, a representative of one of the most disreputable professions. Later on Ando is said to have been pardoned and to have lived to return to Edo, but the date of his death is unclear. Of the many examples surviving, the one reproduced is remarkable for its exquisite color and flair.

11. *Customs of the Twelve Months: June, the Gion Festival*
Important Art Object. Coll. Yamaguchi Hoshun
See Plates 12–15 for other sections from the same series, also note on page 135.

12. *Customs of the Twelve Months: January, New Year's Felicitations*
Important Art Object. Coll. Yamaguchi Hoshun

13. *Customs of the Twelve Months: May, Boys' Festival*
Important Art Object. Coll. Yamaguchi Hoshun

16–23. *Genre Painting Screen*
    Coll. Tokyo National Museum
    Detail from Plate 21 shown in Plate 2, see note, page 135.

14. *Customs of the Twelve Months: August, Moon Viewing*
Important Art Object. Coll. Yamaguchi Hoshun

15. *Customs of the Twelve Months: November, Fire Festival*
Important Art Object. Coll. Yamaguchi Hoshun

24. *Kano Hideyori: Autumn-Foliage Viewing at Takao*
   National Treasure. Coll. Tokyo National Museum. See note, page 135.

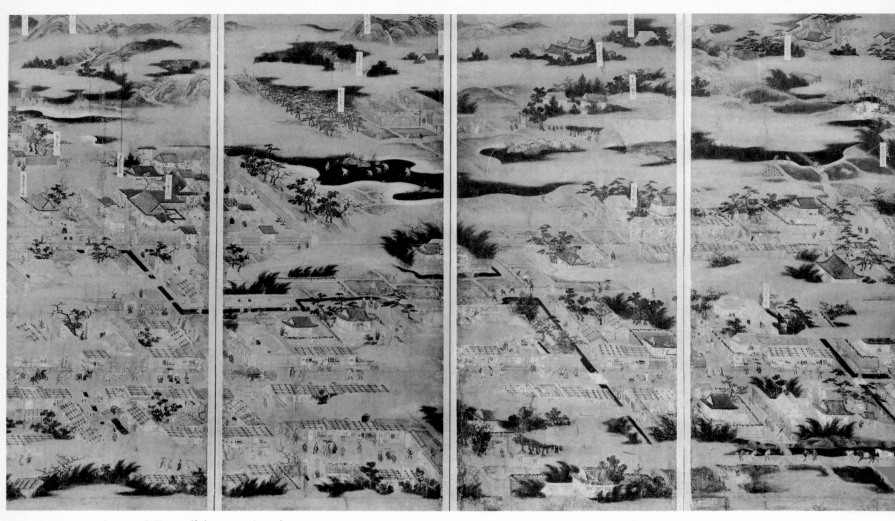

25. *Views in and around Kyoto* (left screen of a pair)
     Important Cultural Property. Coll. Machida Mitsujiro. See note, page 136.

26. *Views in and around Kyoto* (right screen of a pair)
     Important Cultural Property. Coll. Machida Mitsujiro.

27. *Kano Eitoku: Views in and around Kyoto* (left screen of a pair)
     Important Cultural Property. Coll. Uesugi Takanori. See note, page 136.

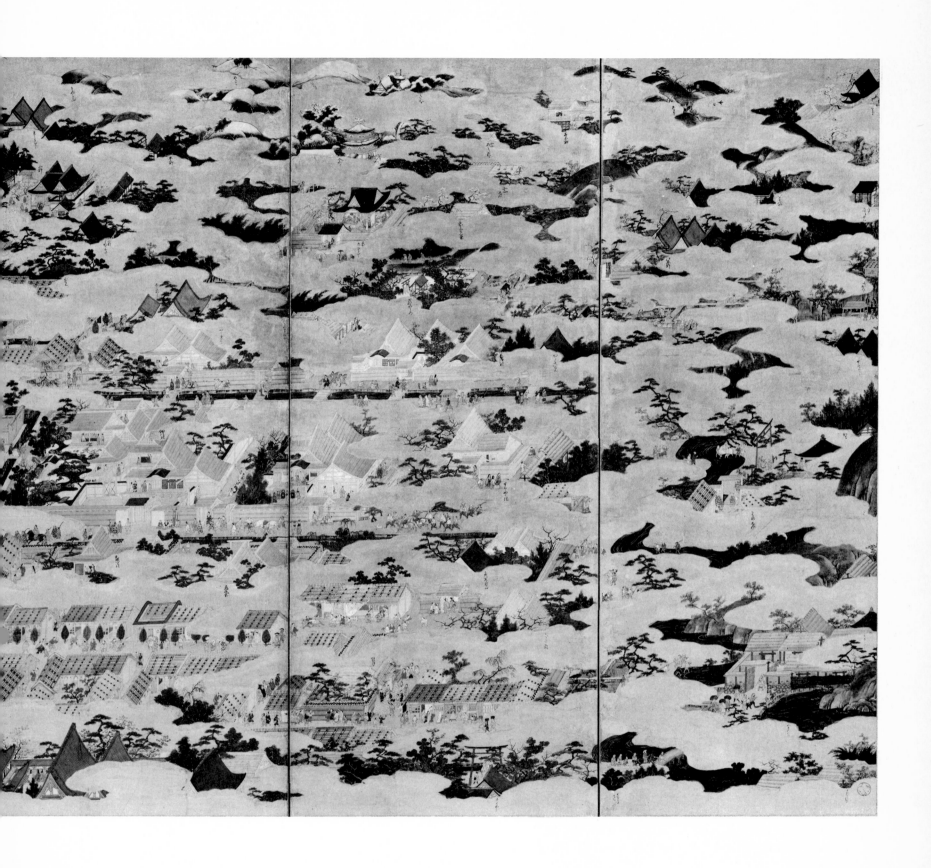

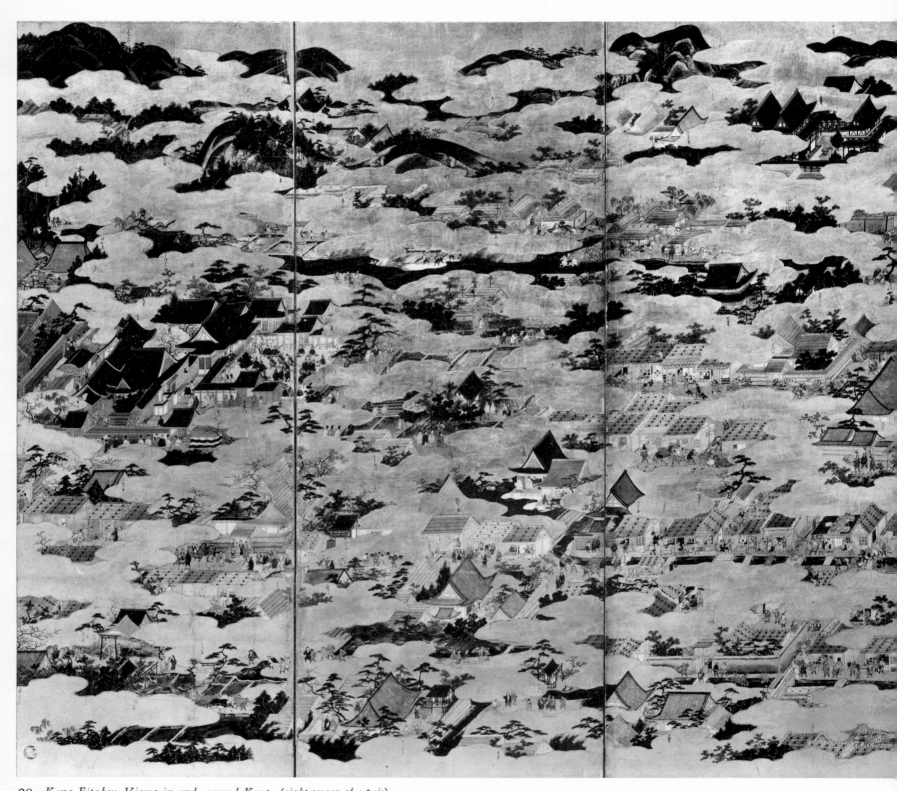

28. *Kano Eitoku: Views in and around Kyoto* (right screen of a pair)
   Important Cultural Property. Coll. Uesugi Takanori.   See note, page 136.

29. *Famous Places in Kyoto* (*left screen of a pair*)
   Coll. anonymous.   See detail in Plate 31, also note, page 137.

30. *Famous Places in Kyoto* (*right screen of a pair*)
   Coll. anonymous.   See detail in Plate 32.

31. *Famous Places in Kyoto (detail from Plate 29)*
    Coll. anonymous. See note, page 137.

32. *Famous Places in Kyoto* (detail from Plate 30)
    Coll. anonymous. See note, page 137.

33. *Genre Painting Mounted on Sliding Doors*
   Important Cultural Property. Coll. Emman-in. See note, page 137.

34. *Genre Painting Mounted on Sliding Doors*
Important Cultural Property. Coll. Emman-in.

35. *Genre Painting Mounted on Sliding Doors of Audience Chamber in Nagoya Castle*
Important Cultural Property. Coll. City of Nagoya. See note, page 137.

66

36. *Genre Painting Mounted on Sliding Doors of Audience Chamber in Nagoya Castle*
   Important Cultural Property. Coll. City of Nagoya.

37. *Festival Ceremonies at the Toyokuni Shrine* (*right screen of a pair*)
    Important Art Object. Coll. Reimei-kai.   See note, page 137.

38. *Festival Ceremonies at the Toyokuni Shrine* (left screen of a pair)
     Important Art Object. Coll. Reimei-kai.   See note, page 137.

39. *Kano Naizen: Festival Ceremonies at the Toyokuni Shrine* (*left screen of a pair*)
Important Cultural Property. Coll. Toyokuni Shrine. See note, page 138.

40. *Kano Naizen: Festival Ceremonies at the Toyokuni Shrine (right screen of a pair)*
Important Cultural Property. Coll. Toyokuni Shrine. See note, page 138.

41. *Views of Artisans: Sword Maker*
    Coll. Okazoe Misao.   See note, page 138.

42. *Views of Artisans: Armorer*
    Coll. Okazoe Misao

43. *Views of Artisans: Fan Maker*
    Coll. Okazoe Misao

44. *Views of Artisans: Furrier*
    Coll. Okazoe Misao

45. *Kano Yoshinobu: Views of Artisans, Spinner*
Important Cultural Property. Coll. Kita-in. See note, page 138.

46. *Kano Yoshinobu: Views of Artisans, Embroiderer*
Important Cultural Property. Coll. Kita-in.

47. *Kano Yoshinobu: Views of Artisans, Weaver*
Important Cultural Property. Coll. Kita-in.

48. *Kano Yoshinobu: Views of Artisans, Fan Maker*
Important Cultural Property. Coll. Kita-in.

49. *Kano Yoshinobu: Views of Artisans, Fabric Printers*
Important Cultural Property. Coll. Kita-in.   See note, page 138.

50. *Flower Viewing and Falconry* (*detail from Plate 52*)
   Important Art Object. Coll. Atami Museum of Fine Art.   See note, page 139.

51. *Flower Viewing and Falconry* (*left screen of a pair*)
    Important Art Object. Coll. Atami Museum of Fine Art. See note, page 139.

52. *Flower Viewing and Falconry* (*right screen of a pair*)
    Important Art Object. Coll. Atami Museum of Fine Art. See detail in Plate 50.

53. *Kano Naganobu: Pleasures under the Blossoms*
    National Treasure. Coll. Hara Kunizo. See detail in Plate 3, also note, page 32.

54. *Tethered Horses* (*left screen of a pair*)
Important Art Object. Coll. Tokyo National Museum. See note, page 139.

55. *Tethered Horses* (*right screen of a pair*)
Important Art Object. Coll. Tokyo National Museum.

56. *Screen with Equestrian Figures* (left screen of a pair)
    Important Cultural Property. Coll. Daigo-ji. See note, page 139.

57. *Screen with Equestrian Figures* (right screen of a pair)
    Important Cultural Property. Coll. Daigo-ji.

58. *A Dog-Baiting Meet* (left screen of a pair)
    Important Cultural Property. Coll. Sugawara Tsusai. See note, page 139.

59. *A Dog-Baiting Meet* (right screen of a pair)
    Important Cultural Property. Coll. Sugawara Tsusai.

60. *Festival Ceremonies at the Kamo Shrine* (*left screen of a pair*)
Important Cultural Property. Coll. anonymous. See note, page 140.

61. *Festival Ceremonies at the Kamo Shrine* (*right screen of a pair*)
Important Cultural Property. Coll. anonymous.

62. *"Southern Barbarians" Screen (left screen of a pair)*
    Coll. Tokyo National Museum.   See note, page 140.

64. *"Southern Barbarians" Screen (left screen of a pair)*
    Coll. Kobayashi Chu.   See note, page 140.

63. *"Southern Barbarians" Screen* (*right screen of a pair*)
     Coll. Tokyo National Museum.

65. *"Southern Barbarians" Screen* (*right screen of a pair*)
     Coll. Kobayashi Chu.

93

66. *The River Bed at Shijo* (*left screen of a pair*)
Important Cultural Property. Coll. Seika-do. See detail in Plate 4, also note, page 34.

67. *The River Bed at Shijo (right screen of a pair)*
Important Cultural Property. Coll. Seika-do. See detail in Plate 68, also note, page 34.

68. *The River Bed at Shijo* (*detail from Plate 67*)
Important Cultural Property. Coll. Seika-do. See note, page 34.

69. *The River Bed at Shijo* (*detail from Plate 71*)
Important Cultural Property. Coll. Domoto Shiro. See note, page 141.

70. *The River Bed at Shijo*
Coll. Misumi Kazunari.   See note, page 140.

71. *The River Bed at Shijo*
Important Cultural Property. Coll. Domoto Shiro.
See detail in Plate 69, also note, page 141.

72. *The Kiyomizu Temple*
   Important Art Object. Coll. Atami Museum of Fine Art.   See note, page 141.

73. *Screen with Kabuki Scene*
   Important Art Object. Coll. Yamamoto Kiyo-o.   See note, page 141.

74. *Screen with Kabuki Scene* (left screen of a pair)
   Important Art Object. Coll. Otsuga Zenin. See note, page 141.

75. *Screen with Kabuki Scene* (right screen of a pair)
   Important Art Object. Coll. Otsuga Zenin.

76. *Hishikawa Moronobu (?): Screen with Kabuki Scene* (*right screen of a pair*)
Important Art Object. Coll. Tokyo National Museum.   See note, page 142.

77. *Hishikawa Moronobu (?): Screen with Kabuki Scene (left screen of a pair)*
   Important Art Object. Coll. Tokyo National Museum. See note, page 142.

78. *Kabuki Sketchbook Scroll* (detail)
   Important Art Object. Coll. Reimei-kai. See note, page 142.

79. *Okuni Kabuki Scroll* (detail)
   Important Art Object. Coll. Umehara Ryuzaburo. See note, page 143.

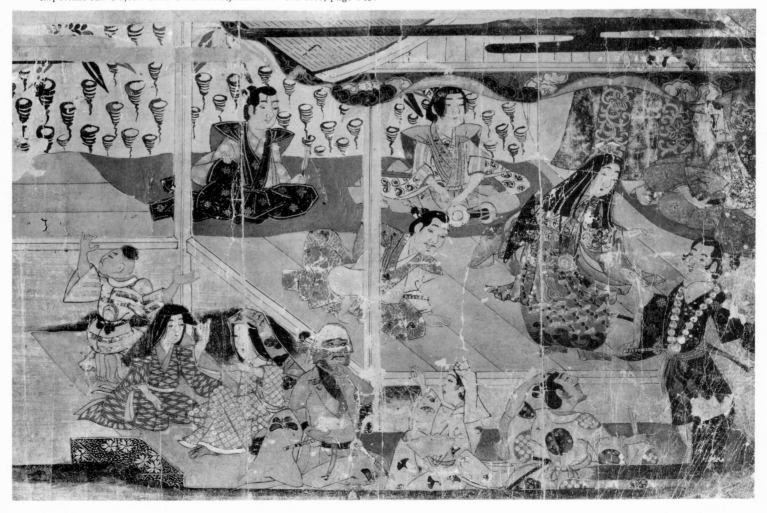

80. *Okuni Kabuki Scroll* (*detail*)
    Important Art Object. Coll. Kyoto University Library. See note, page 143.

81. *The So-o-ji Screen* (*one of a pair*)
    Important Art Object. Coll. Reimei-kai. See note, page 143.
82. *The So-o-ji Screen* (*one of a pair*)
    Important Art Object. Coll. Reimei-kai.

83. *The Weavers*
   Coll. Atami Museum of Fine Art.   See note, page 143.

114

84. *The Rope Door*
    Important Art Object. Coll. Hara Kunizo.   See note, page 143.

85. *Genre Painting*
    Coll. Okazaki Masaomi.   See note, page 143.

87. *Genre Screen with Female Figures*
    Coll. Hosomi Ryoichi.   See note, page 144.

86. *The Gion Festival*
   Coll. Tokyo National Museum.   See note, page 144.

88. The Hikone Screen
National Treasure. Coll. Ii Naochika.   See detail in Plate 1, also note, page 144.

89. *The Pleasures of Women*
    Important Art Object. Coll. Yahata Yotaro.   See detail in Plate 5, also note, page 36.

90. *Dancing Figures*
   Important Art Object. Coll. City of Kyoto. See detail in Plate 7, also note, page 40.

91. *Dancing Figure*
   Coll. Umehara Ryuzaburo. See note, page 144.

92. *A "Kambun Beauty"*
   Coll. Tokyo National Museum. See note, page 144.

93–95. *Genre Figures*
   Coll. Nezu Museum.   See note, page 144.

96. *Honda Heihachiro Portrait Screen*
  Important Cultural Property. Coll. Reimei-kai. See detail in Plate 6, also note, page 38.

97. *The "Pilgrim"*
   Coll. Atami Museum of Fine Art.   See note, page 145.

98. *A Bath Woman*
   Coll. Nakamura Gakuryo.   See note, page 145.

99. *A "Kambun Beauty"*
Coll. Ujiie Takeo. See note, page 145.

100. *Dancing Courtesan?*
Coll. Tokyo National Museum. See note, page 145.

101. *Male Dancer*
Coll. Atami Museum of Fine Art. See note, page 145.

127

102. *Okumura Masanobu: The Ogura Mountain Villa*
Coll. Tokyo National Museum.   See note, page 145.

103. *Hishikawa Moronobu: Beauty Looking over Her Shoulder*
Coll. Tokyo National Museum. See note, page 146.

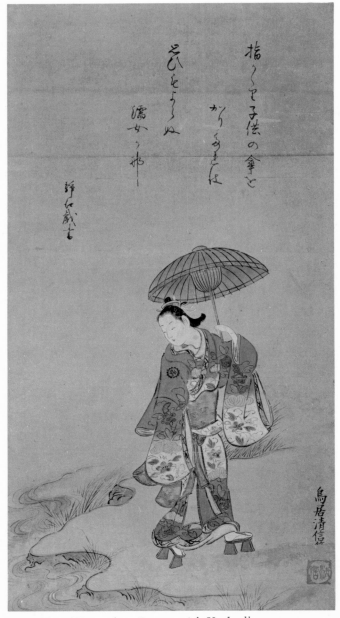

104. *Torii Kiyonobu: Beauty with Umbrella*
Coll. Tokyo National Museum.   See note, page 146.

105. *Nishikawa Sukenobu: Beauty at Her Toilet*
Coll. Atami Museum of Fine Art. See note, page 146.

106. *Tosen-do Rifu: Standing Beauty*
Coll. Tokyo National Museum. See note, page 146.

107. *Miyagawa Choki: Courtesan Enjoying Incense*
Coll. Tokyo National Museum. See note, page 146.

108. *Miyagawa Choshun: Female Figure*
Important Art Object. Coll. Yamato Bunka-kan. See note, page 146.

109. *Miyagawa Choshun: Courtesan Enjoying Incense*
Coll. Tokyo National Museum. See note, page 146.

110. *Hishikawa Moronobu: Genre Scroll* (detail)
     Coll. Tokyo National Museum. See note, page 147.

111. *Miyagawa Choshun: Genre Scroll* (detail)
     Coll. Tokyo National Museum. See note, page 147.

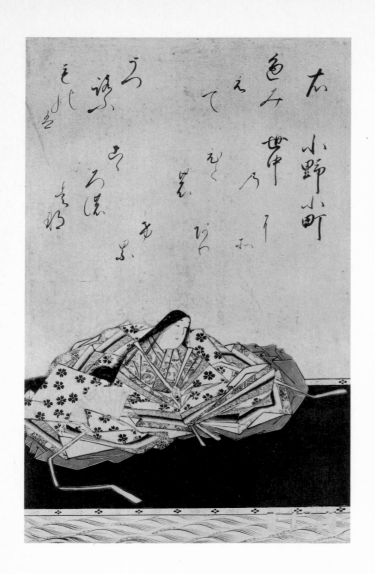

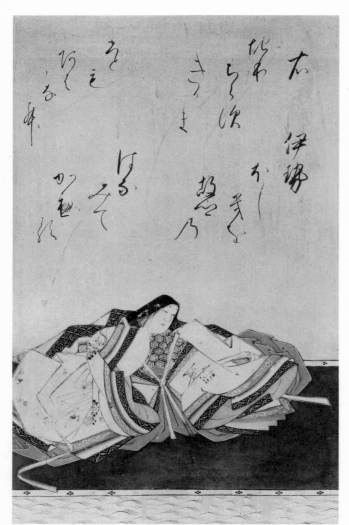

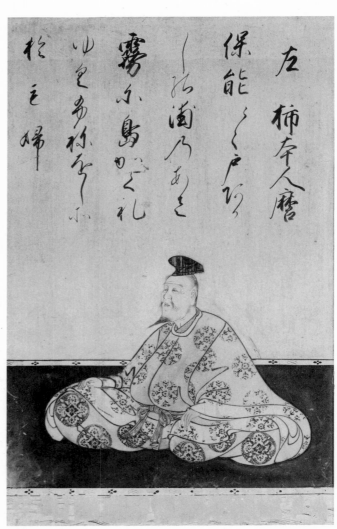

112–15. *Iwasa Katsumochi: The Thirty-six Poets; Ono no Komachi, Narihira, the Poetess Ise, Kakinomoto no Hitomaro*
Important Cultural Property. Coll. Tosho-gu. See note, page 147.

116. *The Horie Romance Scroll* (*detail*)
   Coll. Atami Museum of Fine Art.
   See note, page 147.

117. *Lady Tokiwa Scroll* (*detail*)
   Coll. Atami Museum of Fine Art.
   See note, page 147.

118. *The Oguri Hangan Romance Scroll*
   (*detail*). *Coll. The Imperial Family.*
   See note, page 147.

119. *The Princess Joruri Romance Scroll*
   (*detail*). *Coll. Atami Museum of Fine Art.*
   See note, page 148

Notes on the Plates

11–15. CUSTOMS OF THE TWELVE MONTHS
Important Art Object. Coll. Yamaguchi Hoshun
Colors on paper. Booklet; each panel 32.72×27.87 cm.

Annual festivals and observances were employed as important subject matters for Japanese painting as early as the Heian period (794–1185), and hence often found their way into art for interior decorative purposes. Today, of course, none of these early works survive, but it may be guessed that they were concerned with annual observances among the court nobles and other upper-class members of society.

In the early part of the sixteenth century such pictures began to be produced again, but this time their subject matter was not so much aristocratic observances as it was the everyday activities of the majority of the public. As a result they soon developed into a distinctive type of genre painting. The work reproduced here is one of the oldest surviving ones showing plebeian festivals and observances.

Such activities among the lower levels of society are of course much subject to fads, and tend to be carried out in different ways at different times and in various places. From internal evidence of this sort it is possible to date the present work at somewhere in the last half of the sixteenth century. The screen has scenes for each of the twelve months, in order as follows:

January, New Year's Felicitations; February, Nightingale Song Contests; March, Cockfights; April, Flower Selling; May, Boys' Festival; June, the Kyoto Gion Festival; July, A Fashionable Scene; August, Moon Viewing; September, Autumnal Festival; October, Maple Viewing; November, Fire Festival; December, Playing in the Snow.

Illustrated here are the June episode, showing the Gion Festival procession in Kyoto's ancient gay quarter (Plate 11), and on pages 50 & 51, from the left, the following: for January, a scene of traditional New Year amusements and activities, including a game of battledore and shuttlecock and a dance of felicitation; for May, the Boys's Festival, with young boys engaging in armed jousting; and for August, a scene showing persons gathering the pampas-grass fronds and lespedeza which are used as ceremonial offerings during the moon-viewing parties customarily held during the full moon at this time of year. Finally, in the scene for November a Fire Festival is shown, with persons running about holding lighted torches.

The artist is unknown, but he appears to have been someone working within the traditions of the Tosa school. He has a distinctive touch in his handling of figures and decorative details, and there is much of the classical in his approach to his subjects.

16–23. GENRE PAINTING SCREEN
Coll. Tokyo National Museum
Colors on paper. Eight-fold screen; each panel 67.27×41.81 cm.
See also Plate 2 for detail.

Here are the eight episodes from among which Plate 2 is reproduced; these eight panels have all been mounted on a single large eight-fold screen, but in spite of this there is but little uniformity of

composition among them. In some cases adjacent panels are to be taken together to form a single unit (this is the case with the detail of the color plate and its neighbor to the left), while in others top and bottom of a single panel have been divided into different compositions with different themes.

From the right, the first panel shows the traditional New Year's game of battledore and shuttlecock. The second, top, shows a party of nobles flower viewing, while the bottom half of the same section shows a plebeian party enjoying the same amusement to the accompaniment of a few drinks.

Panels three and four show the replanting of the rice paddies (the top part of panel three is the detail reproduced in Plate 2).

In the upper half of panel five, one finds the ritual horse racing of the Kamo Shrine in Kyoto; in the bottom half, a busy scene in a tailor's shop. The upper half of panel six shows the artistocratic sport of dog baiting (see the caption for Plates 58 & 59), and the ancient courtly game of football in the bottom.

Panel seven is a mounted hunt at the base of Mt. Fuji, while the eighth shows, on the top, a festival at a Shinto shrine, and at the bottom, a gay snow fight.

In its depiction of the march of the seasons of the year, from the early spring of the New Year's games in the first panel through the festivals and sports of summer and autumn, and down finally to the sport of the winter's snow in the bottom section of the last panel on the left, the screen illustrated here is a major departure in subject matter from the content of the traditional sets of views of annual observances upon which it was ostensibly based. In composition it is unique, and it is the only such example known which uses the interesting technique of setting the activities of the warrior class in the upper sections of the panels off against similar or contrasting activities among the commoners, pictured in the lower sections of the same panels.

The representation of the tailor's shop in the bottom of panel five is the oldest such painting known today, and is invaluable as a source of datum about the nature and arrangement of such shops in the latter half of the sixteenth century. Also noteworthy is the fact that the artist responsible for this screen was not, as often, here working in the style of the Kano school, with its Chinese overtones, but rather in the native tradition of indigenous Japanese painting. This gives the work illustrated additional importance as a landmark in the development of Japanese genre art.

24. KANO HIDEYORI: AUTUMN-FOLIAGE VIEWING AT TAKAO
National Treasure. Coll. Tokyo National Museum
Colors on paper. Six-fold screen; 148.1×362.9 cm.

Takao, near Kyoto, was and still is a favorite spot for viewing the colorful autumn foliage in which Japan is so rich, especially the bright scarlet leaves of the Japanese maple. In feudal times the area was popular with both the warrior class and the commoners, and the exquisite six-fold screen illustrated here is a memorable representation of a group of such persons enjoying the loveliness of autumn at this famous site.

Some are eating their lunches which they have brought with them; others enjoy a drink of rice wine. A mother nurses her child, while a man buys a cup of tea from a wandering peddler. And as the eye travels from this charming plebeian scene on the extreme right, it finds it complimented on the extreme left by a group of upper-class persons drinking, dancing, and no doubt singing noisily in unison.

In the central portion another quieter group on the tiny bridge is quietly appreciating the glories of this splendid autumn day, while one of the party plaintively plays on a bamboo flute. All this is of the very essence of genre art, as the artist gives full reign to all his talents in depicting this rich variety of scenes, all upon the theme of enjoying the beauties of nature in autumn.

The artist, Kano Hideyori, is one from whom there are in addition to the present screen few if any known surviving works, but he is said to have been the second son of Kano Motonobu, and to have been active about 1540. Hence the present screen is probably to be dated in the first half of the sixteenth century, and is as a result one of the earliest of such examples of genre art in Japan.

It is interesting to note, in addition, the snow-covered distant mountains in the upper left; these would appear to indicate that the present screen was originally meant to cover the two seasons of autumn and winter, and that once it formed the second half of a set devoted to the four seasons of the year.

The traditional patterns and themes for sets of pictures devoted to annual observances and the four seasons were established in Japanese painting as early as the eleventh and twelfth centuries; the Kano school, for example, to which Hideyori, the artist of the present screen, belonged, counted among its especial traditions the painting of sets of bird-and-flower views against backgrounds of the four seasons.

Hence, as these artists began to be active in genre painting, they naturally came to it against the background of their traditional training, and worked at it initially in terms of the customary themes and materials of their schools. As genre painting in the sixteenth century and after begins to grow in stature in Japan, the story is largely one of its struggle to fight free from the limitations imposed by these impressive traditions. Not until it has struggled to set itself completely free from the restrictions of these traditional forms and themes does genre painting genuinely come of age.

25–26. VIEWS IN AND AROUND KYOTO

Important Cultural Property. Coll. Machida Mitsujiro
Colors on paper, gold ground. Pair of six-fold screens; each screen 137.8×348.4 cm.

Many early examples are known today of large screens which, like the set illustrated, show in minute detail the streets and buildings of the ancient imperial capital of Kyoto, and often much of the surrounding countryside in addition. The one shown here is thought to be the earliest such extant, and may be dated somewhere in the vicinity of 1520. Screens such as this were at the time produced somewhat as souvenirs or mementos of the great city, and probably found their most active sales in provincial areas far removed from the splendid buildings and vistas they pictured.

Almost all these early examples follow the same general scheme of composition; they "read," as it were, from top to bottom, and present a virtual map of the chief buildings, streets, and other landmarks of the city proper and its immediate outskirts.

Many tiny stylized cloud patterns isolate one section from another, while the buildings and the streets are customarily executed, as here, with infinite attention to precision of detail and accuracy of representation. The "guide map" nature of such screens is further emphasized by the fact that in most cases, as here, the important buildings, shrines, temples, and the like are labelled with cartouches bearing the name of each.

Here in the extreme right of the left screen of the pair (Plate 25) can be seen, among many others, two buildings still surviving in Kyoto: the Sanjusangen-do and the large, scaffold-like structure of the Kiyomizu Temple (see the caption of Plate 72). Farther down are the buildings of the imperial palace and the residences of important military figures and nobles of the day.

Scattered among these more imposing structures are the meaner dwellings of the commoners and the buildings housing their shops, often with rocks weighting down their flimsy roofs. Here the busy shopping and amusement areas of a later period in Kyoto's history are not yet evident, another indication of the relatively early date of the work illustrated.

Most similar views of Kyoto are the works of artists working in the tradition of one of the Chinese-style schools of painting, but in the present example the technique is rather that of the Japanese-style Tosa school. The screen illustrated is, as a matter of fact, traditionally ascribed to Tosa Mitsunobu.

27–28. KANO EITOKU: VIEWS IN AND AROUND KYOTO
Important Cultural Property. Coll. Uesugi Takanori
Colors on paper, gold ground. Pair of six-fold screens; each screen 159.4×363.3 cm.

This is a somewhat later example than the Machida Collection screen of the previous plate, and limits itself largely to the buildings and streets of Kyoto proper. The left screen of the set (Plate 27) is devoted to scenes in the western section of the city and the right one (Plate 28) to the east, including the Gion quarter. Here the annual Gion Festival is in progress, its tall, boat-like floats being hauled through the narrow streets in this annual observance.

In the present set of screens Kyoto's streets are seen as they appeared before the military ruler Toyotomi Hideyoshi made certain far-reaching changes in the layout of the ancient capital; this makes possible a fairly certain dating for the set at somewhere before 1570.

The tradition is that the present set of screens was painted by Kano Eitoku on a commission by Oda Nobunaga, the military ruler of Japan who followed Hideyoshi, and that they were presented by Nobunaga to Uesugi Kanenobu, to impress this provincial leader with the glories and prosperity of the southern capital.

Certainly the screens themselves, at present still in the collection of the Uesugi family, lend the necessary air of verisimilitude to this tradition, for they have been executed in the most lively way possible, with lavish use of gold leaf and strikingly impressive colors. The total effect was well calculated to dazzle the eye of any rural noble, unaccustomed as he must have been to the bewildering glories of Japan's ancient center of courtly culture.

Comparison of the set here illustrated with the example in the previous plate from the Machida Collection points up the fact that here the shopping and amusement streets of Kyoto are shown far more lively and more developed; a far larger number of human figures has also been introduced into the present screen. Thus comparison of the two screens shows much of the rapid development of the city which came about in the sixteenth and early seventeenth centuries, with the coming of relative political stability after literally centuries of civil unrest.

Also, again in contrast to the Machida Collection screen, the present set is the work of a first-rate artist painting in the Kano school tradition. This is a valuable indication of how early genre representations began to be important subjects for the leading painters of sixteenth- and seventeenth-century Japan.

29–30. FAMOUS PLACES IN KYOTO
Coll. anonymous
Colors on paper, gold ground. Pair of six-fold screens; each screen 162.7×342.4 cm. See Plates 31 & 32 for details.

By type, the present work actually belongs under the classification "Views in and around Kyoto," but its title derives from the fact that it is concerned entirely with things to be seen within the city proper. Similar works from the Machida and Uesugi collections have much of the classical in their style, but the present example is by contrast with them especially rich in the characteristic elements of sixteenth- and seventeenth-century genre painting.

It is distinctive in its layout, arranging its subject obliquely from the upper left hand corner on down, rather than viewing it head on. Also worthy of note is the way in which both the right and left screens are used in a single connected composition. The bustle and hurry of the ancient capital's crowded streets are cleverly brought out, and literally thousands of individual figures have been introduced to the scene.

The artist's style has certain distinctive features, especially in the thick lips and long, thin faces of the figures, traits linking him with the style of the Iwasa Matahei school. Probably the present work was executed by a journeyman painter with connections with the Iwasa Matahei school, sometime between 1622 and 1624.

This dating is possible from the internal evidence offered by the buildings shown standing at the crossing of the Kamo River bed and Shijo Avenue. Here are found four Kabuki theaters and two marionette theaters, which it is known were placed here sometime after 1622. Furthermore, the Nijo Castle is shown (extreme left, Plate 29) as it was before certain changes and repairs were made to it in 1624, so the assumption is that at the latest the present work was executed before this last date. Further consideration of this variety makes possible the assumption that around 1624 is the most likely date for the work as a whole.

Kyoto itself was in a most flourishing state at this period. The Kabuki theaters at the Shijo river crossing were of course very active, but in addition it was a period when a great variety of amusements, entertainments, and festivals were common in the city. These included the annual Gion Festival processions, masquerades, and a variety of busy business enterprises. Among those shown are fan shops (Plate 31), drug shops, tool shops, and footwear dealers. The licensed quarter of Kami-no-machi in Rokujo (Plate 32) is shown so vividly one can almost reach out and touch the many details. All in all, the viewer here finds a fascinatingly detailed panorama of the people of old Kyoto, busy about their business and pleasure, and taking them both very seriously indeed. Many different screens survive of this general type, but the one illustrated here is surely the finest of all those known today.

33–34. GENRE PAINTING MOUNTED ON SLIDING DOORS
Important Cultural Property. Coll. Emman-in
Colors on paper, gold ground. Four panels; each panel 176.96× 116.06 cm.

This remarkable painting is at present in the collection of the Emman-in, a cloister of the celebrated Buddhist temple Mii-dera, at Otsu, on the shores of Lake Biwa. It is, of course, rather remarkable to find a genre painting of this variety in a temple collection, but according to its owners it found its way into the cloister where it is presently preserved by a curious and complicated path.

It is said to have been a gift to the cloister of Emperor Meisho (1623–97), presented in 1647 in connection with repairs to the Kyoto Imperial Palace which the third Tokugawa shogun Tokugawa Iemitsu began to undertake in 1643. Hence interest in it naturally increases when one learns that it seems, according to this attribution, to have once been a part of the sliding panel decorations of the Kyoto Imperial Palace. In their present condition both of the panels are very much damaged, but their style makes it possible to assign them a fairly early date.

The panels illustrated show scenes along the beach at Sumiyoshi, with a glimpse of the Sumiyoshi Shrine in the far distance, and in the foreground various scenes of everyday life including a game of Japanese chess, eating, and cooking. The damaged portions have caused the heavy colors to drop off (as in the cloud pattern of the left panel), revealing in places the heavy black underpainting, and affording a valuable if accidental glimpse of the artist's working technique.

35–36. GENRE PAINTING MOUNTED ON SLIDING DOORS OF AUDIENCE CHAMBER IN NAGOYA CASTLE
Important Cultural Property. Coll. City of Nagoya
Colors on paper. Eight panels; each panel 162.72×180.90 cm.

These panels were originally in the reception chamber of the Nagoya Castle. The castle itself was destroyed by incendiary bombing during World War II, but fortunately these paintings escaped destruction. The reception chamber of Nagoya Castle was completed in 1614, and these sliding panel paintings probably date from this same time. Such a reception chamber would have been used for the formal assemblies of warriors from the provinces, and it is extremely interesting to find that genre painting of this sort was used in such settings.

The panels show scenes at a boat landing in Sakai, including a festival at Oshima Shrine and agricultural activities, against a landscape background of major proportions. In many ways it is stylistically allied with the panels from the Emman-in (Plates 33 & 34). Unlike, for example, many of the works showing scenes in and around the ancient capital, the present work does not concentrate upon human figures but instead devotes its chief attention to the depiction of a majestic Nature, in which figures are then introduced going about their everyday tasks, as of secondary interest. Such works must have seemed, among the various genre techniques possible, to be especially suitable for the decoration of rooms for official and military functions. In the left of the sections shown here some peasants are quarrelling, while in the right the fields are being planted to the accompaniment of traditional songs.

37–38. FESTIVAL CEREMONIES AT THE TOYOKUNI SHRINE
Important Art Object. Coll. Reimei-kai
Colors on paper. Pair of six-fold screens; each screen 167.2× 352.6cm.

In 1598 the sometime military ruler of Japan Toyotomi Hideyoshi died. He was then installed as a popular deity in the Toyokuni Shrine in Kyoto, and on the seventh year of his death this shrine was the scene of a vast festival to commemorate his spirit.

The people of Kyoto, always partial to festivals and celebrations, appear to have celebrated this one with an enthusiasm remarkable even for the ancient city. The city was divided into sections, and each section sent representatives to the celebration. Costumed in special outfits, these representatives performed a great open-air dance devised for the festival.

In addition, many other special activities took place. Records of the time tell of performances of various types of traditional music and dancing, and of long processions of Shinto priests and warriors in full regalia. Furthermore, on the day following these Toyokuni Shrine celebrations elaborate mass dances were performed in the front of the Great Buddha Image Hall, in the precincts of the Hoko-ji, a Buddhist temple next door to the Toyokuni Shrine.

The present work gives vivid pictorial expression to these lively events, and together with another similar piece preserved to this day in the Toyokuni Shrine itself, it serves as a priceless source of information about the events of the time. In the right section (Plate 37) are to be found the group dances before the Hoko-ji, a scene of quarrelling among the assembled crowds, and several minor dance scenes. These Toyokuni Shrine festival screens are unique among others of the same general type for the skill with which they have handled their large number of busy figures; looking at them it is easy to see just how impressive the eye-witness artist must himself have found the original spectacle.

The left portions (Plate 38) show the music and dance offerings being performed before the Toyokuni Shrine, with dancing by traditionally garbed warriors in attendance. In comparison with other similar works by Kano Naizen, the present one clearly devotes exceptional attention to capturing the vigorous movements of the dancing figures, and thanks to this the entire composition is enfused with a sense of vital motion and action. Heavy, thick colors have been employed over the entire surface, making it a typical example of the genre art of the sixteenth and seventeenth centuries.

39—40. KANO NAIZEN: FESTIVAL CEREMONIES AT THE TOYOKUNI SHRINE

Important Cultural Property. Coll. Toyokuni Shrine
Colors on paper. Pair of six-fold screens; each screen 166.9 × 362.0 cm.

This is another important work devoted to the celebrations commemorating Hideyoshi held in 1604 at the Toyokuni Shrine. The similar work in the collection of the Reimei-kai is also shown (Plates 37 & 38), but the present work is the more impressive of the two. This is no doubt because it was executed by one of the leading artists of the day, Ichio Naizen, a member of the Kano school who had at one time served Hideyoshi. Naizen was a disciple of Shoei, who belonged to the main line of the Kano tradition, and specialized in genre scenes of this variety. He died in 1616 at the age of forty-seven.

The Reimei-kai example is anonymous and far less well executed, which leads one to assume that it is the work of one of the nameless journeymen painters of the period.

The present work presents the dancing in front of the Hoko-ji in a quiet, dignified manner, and lacks the clutter and excitement of the Reimei-kai piece. Much the same is true of its treatment of the music and dancing being performed in front of the Toyokuni Shrine, which in the present work is depicted in a solemn and majestic fashion.

The present work was executed by Naizen to a commission by Katagiri Ichimasa, and was presented to the Toyokuni Shrine two years after the celebrations which it commemorates, in 1606. No doubt this fact helps explain the solemnity and order of its design and execution.

41—44. VIEWS OF ARTISANS

Coll. Okazoe Misao
Colors on paper. Ten panels; each panel 59.7 × 40.0 cm.

Pictures of artisans at work, showing members of the lowest

sections of the newly emergent plebeian culture going about their daily tasks, appear to have become popular quite suddenly, and today a fairly large number of examples survive.

The examples illustrated here, from a set in the Okazoe Collection, are fairly recent discoveries, and are especially remarkable in that they have been executed in the native Japanese *(Yamato-e)* style; most of the similar sets of artisan pictures known today are in the style of the Kano school.

In the Okazoe examples the draftsmanship is already fairly well on its way to later sweeping simplification, and hence they can hardly be thought to have served as models for the copying of other sets.

In the examples illustrated, the scenes shown are (from upper left) a sword maker, an armorer, a fan maker, and a furrier; the four shown are from among the ten that remain from the twenty-four in the original set.

45—49. KANO YOSHINOBU: VIEWS OF ARTISANS

Important Cultural Property. Coll. Kita-in
Colors on paper. Twenty-four paintings mounted on a pair of six-fold screens; each painting 57.5 × 43.6 cm.

The set of artisan views from which five are illustrated here is remarkable on two scores: it is one of the very few such sets which exist today with all twenty-four paintings complete, and at the same time it is one of the few whose authorship is certain. It is a representative work from the brush of Kano Yoshinobu, and shows a sureness of line not to be seen in the similar sets from the Okazoe and other collections.

For some time it has been conjectured that the screens from which these details are illustrated had served as the original for most of the other known sets of such artisan views, but careful comparison with the examples in the Maekawa Collection (not shown in the present volume) indicates that this is not possible, for the present set, from the Kita-in Collection, is clearly copied from the Maekawa set, and hence both these examples rather go back to some third, presently unidentified original.

The affiliation of the various sets of such artisan pictures known to be in existence in different collections today is an extremely vexing problem, and one in which it is often virtually impossible to give definite answers, but in this instance the secondary relation of this Kita-in set to the Maekawa example is clear. Perhaps also the Okazoe set is a copy of this Kita-in group.

In the Kita-in set, the twenty-four paintings have been mounted on a set of two six-fold screens, and show at their work the following artisans of the period:

Buddhist religious-goods makers, umbrella makers, arrow makers, armorers, writing-brush makers, scroll mounters and paper hangers, spinners, leggings makers, fan makers, spear makers, sword sharpeners, mat makers and barrel coopers, bow makers, swordsmiths, rosary stringers, carpenters, quiver makers, inlaid-lacquer workers, embroiderers, tie-and-dye workers, fabric printers, blacksmiths, weavers, and rush-mat weavers.

The artist, Kano Yoshinobu, was the grandson of Kano Yukinobu and died in 1641 at the age of eighty-nine.

Reproduced here on page 77 are, from upper left, the spinner, the embroiderer, the weaver, and the fan maker. Plate 49 on the following page shows the fabric printers at work. Comparison of the fan maker's shop shown in this set with that illustrated earlier from the Okazoe Collection (Plate 43) makes it clear that the Okazoe Collection example is the copy, indicated among other things by the simplification and sketchiness of its line.

51–52. FLOWER VIEWING AND FALCONRY

Coll. Atami Museum of Fine Art

Colors on paper. Pair of six-fold screens; each screen 142.72× 345.50 cm.

The left screen of this pair is devoted to a hawking scene, showing warriors and retainers in hawking costume, while the right screen shows a group of plebeians engaging in flower viewing. Thus it presents an impressive contrast between the pleasures of the warrior class at the period at which it was executed, and those of the common people. Hawking had long been popular among Japanese warriors, but from about the last quarter of the sixteenth century on it suddenly became even more of a fad, and was extremely popular just about the period when most of the works in the present volume were produced. Hawks were used to take smaller birds and wildfowl, and dogs and nets were employed in hunting down larger game.

The right-hand portion of the screen shows a genre scene of colorfully dressed women dancing and amusing themselves among the rapidly scattering cherry blossoms. Either scene would be interesting enough taken alone, but when contrasted as here—the warriors in their traditional, aristocratic sport of hawking, against the plebeians sporting among the blossoms—the sum is far more than simply the total of the individual parts. The treatment of the hawking scene has about it many of the interesting unrealistic conventions of traditional Japanese painting, which contrast with the essentially "modern" aspect of the plebeian scene.

54–55. TETHERED HORSES

Important Art Object. Coll. Tokyo National Museum

Colors on paper. Pair of six-fold screens; each screen 149.6× 353.9 cm.

In China the horse was a common theme in painting as early as the T'ang dynasty (618–907), while in Japan, it begins to appear in art from the Kamakura period (1185–1333) on. The horse was, of course, of consuming interest to Japan's warrior class at all times, and it is easy to understand their interest in depicting it in art, with a view to handing down to posterity the likeness of especially notable examples of the breed, if for no other reason.

The set of two six-fold screens illustrated shows a splendid example of this kind of art, and indeed, tells as much about the costumes and living arrangements of the grooms and stable attendants as it does about the horses themselves. The composition, with the horses shown tethered in their stables, is one in vogue from the end of the Muromachi period (1333–1573), and other similar examples are common, though few are known in which, like the present one, human figures are also introduced.

The present work follows traditional canons of artistic presentation fairly closely in its treatment of the horses, but in the treatment of the grooms the artist has allowed himself more freedom, resulting in extremely lively genre representations.

The adjacent landscape scenes, with their views of flowering cherry trees and pines, have much in common with the smash and vigor of Momoyama period (1573–1614) decorative art. The figures in the foreground are delightful in the extreme; lively genre art at its best is represented in these scenes of grooms, low ranking warriors, Buddhist priests, and others amusing themselves at games of Japanese chess, as their pet monkey and dogs sport about.

It is rather unusual to find that here, instead of the more traditional Japanese style that would otherwise be expected in a work with this subject matter, the then newly introduced "Chinese" style has been employed. It is also worthy of note that here this "Chinese"

style has been expanded to include the treatment of purely Japanese subjects. This is at the same time an indication of the virtual retirement from the scene of the native Japanese tradition.

56–57. SCREEN WITH EQUESTRIAN FIGURES

Important Cultural Property. Coll. Daigo-ji

Colors on paper, gold ground. Pair of six-fold screens; each screen 153.93×360.6 cm.

Here is a work of majestic scale and magnitude of conception, extending over a pair of six-fold screens and presenting in a carefully but excitingly laid out composition twenty-one individual equestrian figures. It is difficult to find fault with any part of the painting, for both the horses and their riders have been executed with rare skill. The artist has made the figures of the horses even more impressive by leaving the background against which they appear virtually blank, except for a slight green ground; otherwise the figures appear to stand out against empty space.

Within the unlimited space thus presented the horses disport themselves in varied attitudes. Some are cantering, some galloping, others about to rear up. Of especial interest is the single figure farthest to the left in the left-hand screen; he appears to have completed his exercises for the day and to be about to head back to the stables.

The angle at which this figure is set against the composition as a whole is fascinating, and provides a stimulating note of heightened accent against the otherwise completely horizontal line of the total composition. Surely the artist who conceived this detail was no run-of-the-mill painter. Who he was is not known, but from his line and style it may safely be assumed that he was some first-rank painter working in the style of the Kano school.

58–59. A DOG-BAITING MEET

Important Cultural Property. Coll. Sugawara Tsusai

Colors on paper, gold ground. Pair of six-fold screens; each screen 152.12×348.4 cm.

The cruel sport of dog baiting was widely practiced among the warrior class in Japan, and appears to have been especially popular from the Kamakura period (1185–1333) on. In the Japanese variety of this pastime, armed men on horseback attempted to hit a dog with bow and arrow. At first it appears to have been engaged in largely with the purpose of encouraging better marksmanship among the warrior class, but in time it degenerated into simply a showy spectacle.

The right-hand one of this pair of six-fold screens shows the scene immediately before the beginning of one of these formal dog-baiting matches. Seventeen equestrian archers are waiting, with drawn arrows, around the periphery of an enormous rope circled on the ground. Inside this rope circle the dog is about to be released.

The left-hand one of the pair shows five mounted archers making after the unfortunate beast, in a scene of rare motion and speed. Here in the building at the extreme left are noble sight-seers and a record keeper. The fact that the sport had by this time become one of the formalized rituals of the warrior class is further emphasized by the way all these spectators are sitting stiffly in formal positions of attention.

As a matter of fact, dog baiting was forbidden on grounds of its cruelty near the end of the Muromachi period (1333–1573), and for a time appears to have been abolished, but it again came into vogue from about the first part of the seventeenth century on. The pair of screens illustrated most likely shows one of the dog-baiting spectacles after this later revival, and though other similar examples are known, the set illustrated is without question the finest treatment of the subject in existence today.

60–61. FESTIVAL CEREMONIES AT THE KAMO SHRINE
Important Cultural Property. Coll. anonymous
Colors on paper, gold ground. Pair of six-fold screens, each screen 153.93 × 357.5 cm.

Ritual horse racing as a part of the annual celebrations at the Kamo Shrine in the outskirts of Kyoto is said to have first been performed in 1093; ever since that time it has continued to be an important and in many ways the most colorful part of the annual festival of this ancient shrine.

The left-hand one of this pair of screens shows a large number of plebeians enjoying themselves in the gardens and spacious wooded grounds of the shrine during the annual festival, while the right screen is devoted to this famous ritual horse racing.

The amount of care which the artist has devoted to the cryptomeria and pine trees which dot the precincts of the shrine is remarkable, as is the skill with which his composition combines these landscape elements with a large number of human figures. In the bottom of the left screen horses and their riders are refreshing themselves in a convenient stream after the exertions of the racing; this charmingly natural scene leads the eye to the other screen of the set with ease and skill.

In the right screen all attention naturally centers on the horse racing, which is at its peak in the area between the two long fences stretching horizontally across the central portion of the composition. Here too much attention has been paid to the careful representation of a large number of human figures, especially the priests, the warriors, and the plebeians who are engrossed in watching the racing.

Many similar sets of screens showing the Kamo Shrine festivals are known today, but the pair illustrated is thought to be one of the earliest. It is free from the later formalization of composition, and the artist has here obviously still felt himself free to arrange and execute his subject matter in a completely unrestrained fashion. This set of screens is also notable since it appears to have been executed not by someone working in the tradition of the Kano school but rather by an artist in the tradition of native Japanese painting.

62–63. "SOUTHERN BARBARIANS" SCREEN
Coll. Tokyo National Museum
Colors on paper. Pair of six-fold screens; each screen 152.6 × 352.8 cm.

The general term "Namban (Southern Barbarian) screens" is applied to a large number of genre screens which have as their chief theme the trade which flourished between Japan and Portugal from the latter part of the sixteenth century on. Some thirty sets of such screens are known to be in existence today, and almost all of them limit themselves in their subject matter to scenes in the ports around which this foreign trade centered.

Most of these screens resemble each other in style and composition so much that it is suspected that most if not all of them are copies of a few originals, no doubt the work of some of the journeymen painters engaged in artistic "mass production."

Roughly, the screens of this type surviving today can be divided into three main categories:

1. Those where the left screen shows a foreign boat coming into port and unloading its cargo and the right one shows processions through the port of the foreign sailors and traders, their contacts with Japanese, the welcoming of missionaries, and similar scenes.

2. Those where the left screen shows foreign port scenes and the right one shows foreign vessels entering a Japanese port, unloading cargo, and processions. Thus sets of this type handle on a single screen those themes which sets of the first variety divide between the right and left screens.

3. Screens where the right screen shows boats entering port, unloading cargoes, and processions, while the left shows foreigners racing horses, dancing, and engaging in other everyday activities.

The set illustrated is one of this third variety, with horse racing on the left screen, and various scenes connected with Japan's early foreign trade on the right.

64–65. "SOUTHERN BARBARIANS" SCREEN
Coll. Kobayashi Chu
Colors on paper. Pair of six-fold screens; each screen, 153.6 × 363.8 cm.

As explained in the caption to Plates 62 & 63, above, it is possible to divide most of the "Namban screens" known today into three general groups. According to this scheme the set illustrated here belongs to the first group.

The left screen shows a Portuguese boat entering a Japanese harbor and cargo being unloaded. The right one shows foreigners landing, coming into the city, and being welcomed by the Japanese. Since the trade with Portugal at the time was largely restricted to Nagasaki, it is safe to assume that the present set of screens pictures scenes taking place there. However, since in their execution there is a good deal of decorative formalism, especially in the gold-leaf clouds and the composition of the buildings, it would be a mistake to assume that we have here a realistic presentation of any particular part of the city of Nagasaki.

Many similar sets are known today, a tribute to the energy with which the artists of the day no doubt undertook the mass production of this popular subject. The artist was probably a journeyman painter of the Kano school, and the screens were probably not produced in Nagasaki but more likely in Kyoto, sometime in the thirty-year period beginning in 1600.

70. THE RIVER BED AT SHIJO
Coll. Misumi Kazunari
Colors on paper. Six-fold screen; 74.4 × 271.2 cm.

While the examples of similar pieces from the Seika-do and Domoto collections are both pairs of large screens, the one illustrated here from the Misumi Collection is a single, fairly small six-fold screen. This present screen has only recently been discovered, and while today it is an isolated specimen it is thought that originally it formed the right member of a set of two such screens. Also, in contrast with the free, gentle line of the Seika-do and Domoto examples, the figures and buildings in the present work are considerably miniaturized, pointing to a somewhat later date.

The artist here has devoted his major attention to the entertainments being staged in the shrine precincts and to the Kabuki performances in the bed of the Kamo River; these episodes are centered upon in a striking fashion, but for the rest of his composition he has considerably weakened his own effectiveness by taking refuge at once in expanses of gold-leaf clouds.

One of the remarkable points about the screen illustrated is the scene of Sumo wrestlers to be seen in the lower section of the center portion; this type of scene is rare on such screens, and has great value for the study of contemporary customs.

71. THE RIVER BED AT SHIJO

Important Cultural Property. Coll. Domoto Shiro
Colors on paper; Two-fold screen; 152.2×157.2 cm.
See Plate 69 for detail

Of the four examples of screens showing the entertainments in the Kamo River bed in Kyoto which are known today, the pieces from the Seika-do and Domoto collections most resemble each other. Both are mainly devoted to scenes of the notorious "women's" Kabuki, but also lavish much attention upon the other entertainments, stalls, and shops which flourished in the surrounding areas.

The detail from this screen (Plate 69) shows with lively realism one of the many minor attractions of this plebeian amusement area: "The Armless Lady Archer!" She sits on a mat spread on the ground, holds the bow with one foot and manages to draw the arrow with the other, to shoot it into the straw target opposite. And her audience, though small, is both wrapt in incredulous attention and catholic in composition: young and old, men and women, all the lower orders of Kyoto's teeming population flock to the bed of the Kamo River to enjoy sights of exactly this sort.

Surely both this pathetic cripple and her motley audience would find it hard to believe the immortality which the master of the Domoto Collection screen has here bestowed upon them all.

72. THE KIYOMIZU TEMPLE

Important Art Object. Coll. Atami Museum of Fine Art
Colors on paper. Six-fold screen; 152.42×361.2 cm.

The screen illustrated is unique in showing in a single composition a view of the Kiyomizu Temple, in the hills to the east of Kyoto, and a lively scene of a performance by the "women's" Kabuki. It is also remarkable for the colorful costumes of the many figures it shows.

Many of the men are seen wearing trousers; these were undoubtedly modeled after the trousers that the Portuguese merchants had about that time just introduced into Japan, and must then have been the last word in male fashion. Even the material from which these trousers are made is somehow foreign-looking in its patterns. Some idea of the rapid inroads which the material culture of the West made in Japan is gained by reflecting that the scene shown probably is based upon fact: smart dandies dressed in the latest Portuguese styles and patterns no doubt did strut through the streets of Kyoto in exactly this way!

The Kiyomizu Temple, built in the low, charming hills which fringe Kyoto to the east, is celebrated for its distinctive wooden architecture, and especially for the large, stage-like verandah which overhangs a slight valley. From this the view of the cherry blossoms in spring and the scarlet autumn foliage is justly celebrated.

The temple is somewhat removed from the center of Kyoto, and there is no evidence in contemporary documents that Kabuki stages were ever built as close to it as the present screen would indicate. At the time, all the "women's" Kabuki entertainments were concentrated in the bed of the Kamo River at Shijo, and what is seen here is no doubt a representation of the kind of thing that went on there, not anywhere close to the Kiyomizu Temple, a considerable distance removed from the Shijo crossing of the river.

What the artist has done here is, in other words, to take two scenes widely separated in place and to bring them together into a single unified composition. At first glance this may seem exceptionally forced and unnatural, but it is perfectly within the conventions of Japanese decorative art of the period, and when viewed from within the limits imposed by these conventions, it is not in any way an irrational or unnatural composition.

The artist was interested here in bringing together just those scenes in which he knew his viewers would be interested; geographical or topographical reality could quite easily be sacrificed if necessary to make the desired composition possible.

The Kiyomizu Temple is built among low hills, while the Kabuki performances took place in a dry river bed, but this difference in altitude too could be completely overlooked in the final composition. Such blending together of the totally unlike was also perfectly within the conventions of the art, and neither artist nor patron found anything forced or unreal about the result.

Partly this was because of the skillful way in which trees and clouds are used in compositions of this sort; they help to conceal the most striking anomalies in this bringing together of two totally separate and dissimilar scenes. In its own way, the scene illustrated is therefore something of a textbook on the essential methodology of Japan's decorative art, especially on its composition techniques and conventions.

73. SCREEN WITH KABUKI SCENE

Important Art Object. Coll. Yamamoto Kiyo-o
Colors on paper. Six-fold screen; 87.87×267.87 cm.

Here the artist has devoted his composition to the Kabuki stage and its audience; this is in contrast to those screens of similar subject matter where attention is also lavished upon the other entertainments and shops of the vicinity.

The scene being acted upon the stage is thought to be a bawdy skit in which Okuni, in the role of a young samurai and accompanied by a clown named Saruwaka, sets out to purchase some prostitutes. The primitive Kabuki repertory consisted largely of dances, interspersed as necessary by suggestive skits like the one seen on the stage here.

Among the spectators there are members of the warrior class and townsmen, all evidently enjoying themselves hugely as they watch the stage, play chess, and nibble at their lunches. The spectators in the elevated area are no doubt warriors of relatively high station.

Outside the theater proper can be seen a sweetmeat vendor, his temporary stall protected by an umbrella, the door keepers, and passers-by. The entire scene is executed in a clear, explanatory fashion, and as a result is of course priceless for those interested in the early stages of development of the Kabuki stage and theater.

74–75. SCREEN WITH KABUKI SCENE

Important Art Object. Coll. Otsuga Zenin
Colors on paper. Pair of six-fold screens; each screen 154.6× 343.0 cm.

The left-hand one of this pair of screens shows women amusing themselves with the fashionable pastimes of the day; only the right one is devoted to the Kabuki stage. Originally both these screens were much smaller than in their present mounting, and the expanse of stylized clouds above the roofs in each was added when the pictures were remounted on the present larger frames.

The right screen shows what is technically known as *yaro* or "guys'" Kabuki, concerning which a word of explanation may be in order. Specifically, this term refers to Kabuki performances immediately after 1652, when the government decree forbidding men to take part in Kabuki performances was issued.

Originally women had taken all the roles in the simple dances and bawdy skits which constituted the early Kabuki repertory, but the appearance of women upon the Kabuki stage was strictly forbidden by a decree of 1629, because it was felt that they were having a deleterious effect upon public morals. Since most if not all of the ladies so engaged had been recruited from some of the less respectable of Kyoto's many bawdy houses, official fears in this connection were probably fairly well founded.

Be that as it may, the decree of 1629 did not completely solve the problem of safeguarding public morality in seventeenth-century Japan, for in place of the now-taboo women, troupes of *wakashu* or "young boys'" Kabuki soon were organized. These actors were attractive young men in their early teens, who performed roughly the same repertory of dances and suggestive skits that the ladies whom they replaced had developed.

In their turn, however, these *wakashu* soon became increasingly popular with the homosexual elements in their plebeian audiences, and were themselves forbidden in 1652, again in the hope of preventing any further decay in the standards of public morality.

The government authorities now attempted to do more than simply ban the performances of these high-spirited teenagers; in an attempt to put some measure of a punitive nature into their restriction it ordered that all the *wakashu* performers would have to shave off the forepart of their hair. The performers obeyed at least this part of the law, but then continued to appear on the stage with their partly shaven pates conspicuously wrapped in colorful turbans. What became popular, in their turn, as "guys'" Kabuki were the performances by these shaven, turbaned, but not seriously chastised young actors.

The right screen illustrated shows what is probably the grand finale from a performance by these irrepressible Kabuki veterans; the turbans in which each has swathed his head are clearly visible, as the twenty-one actors come down along the runway extending out into the audience. Probably the representation dates from shortly after the pate-shaving decree of 1652, and the artist was capitalizing on the vogue that these turbaned actors were then enjoying.

In the left screen a number of ladies engage in dignified female amusements, reading, writing, playing chess, and of course gossiping. In common with the actors of the other screen these ladies have a somewhat degenerate air, in their case somewhat heightened by the slightly voluptuous, plump style in which they have been drawn. No doubt this too is a reflection of the slightly decadent taste which set in from about 1650 on.

76–77. HISHIKAWA MORONOBU (?): SCREEN WITH KABUKI SCENE
Important Art Object. Coll. Tokyo National Museum
Colors on paper. Pair of six-fold screens; each screen 170.0 × 387.0 cm.

From about the last decade of the seventeenth century on the Kabuki theater in Japan made rapid progress. This was the period when such great actors as Sakata Tojuro and Ichikawa Danjuro were active, and both in Kyoto and Edo the activities of these and other celebrated figures of the early Kabuki did much to determine the course of its development for all time.

The screen illustrated shows one of the Edo theaters, the Morita-za, as it appeared during the last years of the sixteenth century, with the greenrooms and restaurants which were part of the same building, in a composition of considerable scale and splendor.

In the right screen one sees first the area around the entrance to the theater, lively with the sounds of the barkers as they call to the prospective customers and point out the attractions described on the playbills hung about the doorway. Once inside, we find that a group of women, who appear from their dress and manner to be the wives of members of the warrior class, are enjoying the play from elevated seats, while the general run of play-goers watch it from a pounded earth-floor immediately before the stage.

On the stage an all-male cast, dressed in both male and female attire, is engaged in a colorful dance finale to their production, while upstage one glimpses the musicians with *shamisen* and drums.

The left screen shows the interior of the greenroom, with actors putting on their make-up, dressing their hair, changing costumes, and in general participating in a scene of busy activity.

Further along to the left there is a scene in a small restaurant attached to the theater, where several groups are shown at a party in the company of male actors in female costume.

The screen is unsigned, but it is traditionally ascribed to Hishikawa Moronobu. Judging from the style of certain details in the painting, it is probably by someone allied to the Hishikawa line, or at least working in its tradition.

78. KABUKI SKETCHBOOK SCROLL
Important Art Object. Coll. Reimei-kai
Colors on paper. Horizontal scroll; 37.0 × 1569.5 cm.

This scroll is traditionally believed to depict a scene in one of the earliest types of Kabuki theater, during the first period of its development when all the roles were still enacted by women. The scroll itself, however, is surely not as old as its subject matter would indicate, and no doubt presents the scene in a retrospective or reminiscent fashion. From the entrance we are led into the audience, then to the stage, and finally backstage, in visual episodes full of precious data about the earliest stages of this distinctive Japanese theater art.

The draftsmanship is distinguished by a soft, easy line, and the whole executed in heavy colors and gold leaf, to produce a rich, splendid effect. The artist certainly has an individual style, but unfortunately nothing is known about him.

It is interesting to note that there are Portuguese visitors pictured among the spectators at the play, and also that the audience includes several "modern" Japanese gentlemen sporting Western clothing and puffing away at their pipes. It would appear that at the time social intercourse between Portuguese and Japanese was comparatively free and relaxed, and that it was possible for them to come together at entertainments of the type here pictured.

On stage the chief female performer stands in the center, resting on a decorated sword in an ornate scabbard, of a type that was the rage at the time; she is colorfully dressed and wears a crucifix on a chain about her neck. Accompanying her in the skit being performed are two other actresses, one dressed as a man and carrying a portable chair on her back. The crucifix, of course, does not indicate that either the actress or the role she is playing were Christians, but was merely a fashionable female accessory of the period, for we know from contemporary evidence of the period that the fashion of wearing such ornaments was widely in vogue and had nothing to do with the newly introduced Christian religion. Here, as always, the Kabuki stage has been quick to seize upon the fashion and fad of the moment. The scene is almost identical with that shown in Plate 73, thought to be of Okuni and a clown called Saruwaka.

The scroll, of which only a portion is illustrated here, is an exceptionally long one, and deals in considerable detail with all aspects of Kabuki.

79. OKUNI KABUKI SCROLL

Important Art Object. Coll. Umehara Ryuzaburo
Colors on paper. Horizontal scroll; 18.48 × 27.27 cm.

This is a detail from a celebrated scroll that was famous already during the Edo period (1614–1868); its archaic style of draftsmanship testifies for an early date. On stage is the foundress of the Kabuki art, Okuni. Her performance is being watched by a handful of spectators, when up from the audience rises the ghost of her dead lover, Nagoya Sanzo, to address her.

The love story of Okuni and Sanzo was celebrated in early Kabuki, and was worked into many of the early, fairly primitive stage presentations. Surely the conceit of, as here, continuing the story beyond the grave and having Okuni on stage addressed by the ghost of her lover, speaking to her from among the audience, must have fascinated the spectators in the early days of the art.

In addition, the present scroll contains the libretto for the music used in Okuni's dance in the skit illustrated.

80. OKUNI KABUKI SCROLL

Important Art Object. Coll. Kyoto University Library
Colors on paper. Horizontal scroll; 13.5 × 16.0 cm.

This is a detail from an extremely simple illustrated volume in which drawings of archaic style alternate with sections of text. Okuni was a priestess of the Grand Shrines of Izumo who is supposed to have begun the dance performances which later developed into the Kabuki theater, first appearing in the precincts of the Kitano Shrine in Kyoto.

Here she is seen on stage, wearing an umbrella-like hat and holding a small bell in one hand, which she strikes with a mallet held in the other to keep the time for her dance. Looking at her as she is pictured here it is easy to understand how the word Kabuki came to be used for the theater genre which she is supposed to have founded; it comes, after all, from an archaic verb *kabuku* meaning "to cavort or fool about," and here certainly fits this peculiar figure on stage, in her costume which is neither thoroughly male nor thoroughly female.

From simple performances like the one pictured it was only a short step to the regular theater stalls which soon sprang up in the dry river bed at Shijo Avenue, in Kyoto, to be seen in other works reproduced in the present volume. The text sections in the volume of which a detail is reproduced here are identical with those in the scroll in the Umehara Collection (Plate 79), and another similar one is known in the collection of Mr. Sasaya Inosuke.

81–82. THE SO-O-JI SCREEN

Important Art Object. Coll. Reimei-kai
Colors on paper. Pair of eight-fold screens; each screen 126.36 × 209.0 cm.

The name by which the genre screen here illustrated is often known, the "So-o-ji Screen," is given to it because it is traditionally believed to have been a treasured possession of Okame, the mother of Yoshimasa, founder of the Oshu branch of the Tokugawa house. (After her death Okame was honored under the religious title of So-o-no-In.) It is interesting to reflect that a genre screen of this nature thus appears to have been a prized belonging of a family closely associated with the *de facto* rulers of Japan.

The screen shows plebeian entertainments and amusements both indoors and outdoors, but also pays some attention to the warrior class. Outside there are warriors quarrelling, plebeian picnics, shows, tea houses, boating, dances, and football; inside there are drinking parties, baths, dramatic skits, and many others. There is a delicate, enchanted charm about the draftsmanship and composition which makes the work a virtual embodiment of the essence of genre art.

83. THE WEAVERS

Coll. Atami Museum of Fine Art
Colors on paper. Two-fold screen; 151.2 × 171.2 cm.

A woman is weaving, assisted by her two daughters. A composition of clouds divides the loom scene from the upper portion of the screen, where one female figure prepares cloth for dyeing and another sews. To the right white chrysanthemums bloom in profusion, to the left there is bamboo, above morning glories, and below pampas grass, forming a floral frame for the scene with its figures. Picturing flowering chrysanthemums, as here, using thick applications of Chinese white is a well-known device in decorative painting of the Momoyama period (1573–1614).

The female figures are also distinctive, with their full, even plump, faces and half-opened mouths, typical of the style known popularly as that of Iwasa Matahei. This was a style of figure painting much in vogue around 1620. The present work is surely not from the brush of Matahei himself, the artist after whom this fashionable style was named, but it is nevertheless completely representative of this particular vogue when it was still at the height of its popularity.

84. THE ROPE DOOR

Important Art Object. Coll. Hara Kunizo
Colors on paper. Two-fold screen; 159.69 × 90.30 cm.

The woman who here has quietly reached out her hand to push aside a portion of the rope curtain which hides her from view is a harlot, as can be seen at once from the exaggeratedly elaborate coiffure which she affects. At the time this was a legally recognized trademark of her profession.

But in this exquisite oval face, with its delicately lined eyes and tiny mouth, there is a calm serenity of expression which is strangely impressive, all the more so in view of the essential subject matter treated here. Her kimono has a pattern of flowering wisteria against stylized waves; this, together with the checked design of her obi are in the height of elegant feminine fashion in the first part of the seventeenth century.

Her tiny pet dog, too, is in the highest fashion, for it is a Portuguese variety just then fashionable in Japan. The piece illustrated is the right of a two-fold screen, but the left one shows a bamboo screen and has no connection with the section illustrated. No doubt the original right section was destroyed at some time in the past, and what is in its place at present is no more than a later makeshift, devised in order to complete the set.

85. GENRE PAINTING

Coll. Okazaki Masaomi
Colors on paper. Single panel; 101.81 × 186.96 cm.

This is a busy scene: in the upper left an outdoor party watches dancing in a temporary enclosure formed of lengths of different-colored cloth; in the upper right a young nobleman rides onto the scene surrounded by several menials on foot; below other parties are going on in the buildings surrounding and reaching out over the lake. Other figures are smoking tobacco or refreshing themselves at a penny tea stall. This exceptionally lively work probably dates from sometime around 1640.

86. THE GION FESTIVAL

Coll. Tokyo National Museum

Colors on paper. Six-fold screen; 123.3 × 270.3 cm.

Since so many of the genre paintings of the period treated in this volume were concerned with the lively scenes of festivals and religious celebrations, it is only to be expected that a considerable number of the surviving examples should be devoted to the theme of Kyoto's ancient Gion Festival, one of Japan's most famous and interesting annual celebrations.

Here the broad expanse of a single six-fold screen is devoted to a pictorial representation of the precincts of Kyoto's Gion Shrine, today more usually known as the Yasaka Shrine, about which the annual ritual centers. Gold-leaf clouds are scattered about the sky in a strikingly decorative effect.

The artist has revealed a sharp and observant eye, and he shows in loving detail the many activities of the visitors to the shrine, as they worship in front of the main building, visit the stalls and shops set up in the vicinity, and engage in heated quarrels.

The curious two-storied gate to be seen in the extreme bottom left of the screen is still to be found at the entrance to the Yasaka Shrine in Kyoto; even the two guardian-king figures clearly visible on either side of the gate are still to be seen in the same location.

87. GENRE SCREEN WITH FEMALE FIGURES

Coll. Hosomi Ryoichi

Colors on paper. Six-fold screen; 60.9 × 197.57 cm.

Seen here is a work that is really simply a variation upon the much better known "Hikone Screen" (Plates 1 & 88), with two fewer figures and certain changes in the composition. Several such "variations" upon the famous "Hikone Screen" are known to be in existence, and no doubt are to be credited to the fame of the original work, which has of course inspired many copies and imitations. At the very least, such copies are eloquent testimony to the popularity of the original.

Here the copy is somewhat smaller than the original, reflecting a more plebeian market. The poses of the figures and even details of the line and painting are clearly copied from the original work. The figures of the men added in the copy are poorly done, and show the basic lack of skill of the painter. Probably the work itself is of a relatively late period.

88. THE HIKONE SCREEN

National Treasure. Coll. Ii Naochika

Colors on paper, gold ground. Six-fold screen; 94.0 × 274.8 cm.

See also Plate 1 for detail in color.

This is the famous work usually known in Japan as "The Hikone Screen." Its traditional name derives from the fact that it was for long in the possession of the house of Ito, the hereditary feudal lords of the fief of Hikone. It has been well known in Japan from the middle of the seventeenth century on as a *chef-d'oeuvre* of genre painting. Today many copies of this celebrated screen are known to exist, some indeed famous enough to find their own way into a collection such as the present one; see for example Plate 87.

The detail illustrated in Plate 1, showing a man and a woman playing Japanese checkers while another woman looks on and a young man plays the *shamisen*, is the second section from the left of the screen. The landscape screen which is used as the background for this section of the composition is itself extremely well done, and would appear to be from the brush of some master of the Kano school.

It is of course typical of the conventions surrounding genre painting that even a painter of such skill as the master of "The Hikone Screen" obviously would not sign his name, but here the anonymity of the work may also be explained by the fact that it was probably executed to the commission of some feudal dignitary.

In Japan it has long been the custom that work executed to commissions from the imperial family and other high-ranking parties is not signed. Even without this restriction of custom, however, it would still probably have been considered beneath the dignity of any master of the Kano school to sign his name to a work which, like this, so obviously uses the activities of the lower orders of society for its theme. Japan's feudal society, after all, was intensely interested in keeping the boundaries between the many levels of its society clearly differentiated.

The figures have been executed with great attention to bringing out a slightly decadent elegance quite typical of many genre paintings; here these touches help to emphasize the spirit of happy, unconcerned amusement in which the persons pictured seem quite content to spend their days.

91. DANCING FIGURE

Coll. Umehara Ryuzaburo

Colors on paper, gold ground. Single panel; 62.72 × 35.45 cm.

The screen showing similar dancing figures in the collection of the City of Kyoto (Plate 90) was originally one of a set of two six-fold screens, of which Kyoto today owns only one. The other half of this set is today scattered; four sections have been mounted into a four-fold screen now in the Higuchi Collection, and the remaining two sections, too, are probably still identifiable in various collections. The fragment illustrated here is thought to be one of them; unfortunately it has suffered much at the hands of later restorers, and the coloring is in places muddied as a result.

92. A "KAMBUN BEAUTY"

Coll. Tokyo National Museum

Colors on paper. Single panel; 83.3 × 32.7 cm.

Her left hand holds up the hem of her kimono; her right is hidden within her voluminous sleeve, as she steps out on the narrow veranda which joins directly onto the open room, an expression of infinite elegance on her charming face. Her brilliantly designed costume is typical of that worn by younger women of the warrior class. The work probably dates from shortly after 1660; the decade from 1661 to 1672 was known as the Kambun period, and since the figure illustrated perfectly typifies the ideals of elegant feminine beauty of the period, the work itself is usually known in Japan as "Portrait of a Beauty of the Kambun Period."

93–95. GENRE FIGURES

Coll. Nezu Museum

Colors on paper. Three panels; each panel 76.7 × 30.3 cm.

The center one of these three panels shows a prostitute, with the high coiffure typical of her profession, with a young warrior in each of the two side panels. According to an inscription on the set these are to represent, in the center panel, Okuni, foundress of the Kabuki, with her lover Sanzo on the left and his deadly rival Fuwa Bunzaemon on the right, but this is surely little more than an *ad hoc* explanation added long after the fact by some later hand. There is no reason to believe that Okuni, whatever her other failings may have been, was ever employed as this variety of prostitute.

The central female figure wears a kimono with a design of mill wheels, and is using a toothpick. Her tiny female companion carries a huge *shamisen*. Both are depicted with an easy, voluptuous grace which contrasts in the most effective fashion possible with the strong poses that the two male figures, on the right and left, assume. Also effective is the rhythmic contrast between her elaborate dress and their simple, black and white outfits.

The panels illustrated bear two seal impressions, one circular, the other lozenge-shaped, which can be seen in the lower corners of each. Their exact significance had long puzzled connoisseurs. Some had thought they were signature seals of the artist, others had felt they were placed on the panels by some early owner. Lately, however, it has been discovered that these are the seal impressions of Iehisa, eighteenth in the line of the feudal lords of Shimazu, who died in 1638, and were no doubt placed on the panels while they were still in his possession. It is of course as interesting for the history of art as it is valuable for the history of culture to learn that these panels were once in the collection of one of Japan's most wealthy and influential feudal families.

97. THE "PILGRIM"
Coll. Atami Museum of Fine Art
Colors on paper. Single panel; 37.57 × 18.78 cm.

An air of tenderness pervades the figure of this tiny panel painting, one of the rare examples of a dated painting in the present volume. It bears an inscription dating it in correspondence with 1668. Contemporary documents make it possible to identify the figure as that of a prostitute in a gay quarter of the period known as Katsuyama; on the death of her father she took to wearing the garb of a Buddhist pilgrim as a tribute to his memory, and from this became celebrated as a laudable example of the virtue of filial piety.

In many of the early examples of Japan's genre painting the artists, as in this case, sought to present actual, living persons as their subjects. The present panel is also important since it shows one of the ways in which genre painting tended in time to develop exclusively into paintings of beautiful women.

98. A BATH WOMAN
Coll. Nakamura Gakuryo
Colors on paper. Single panel; 75.0 × 28.0 cm.

This panel shows another bath woman, but this time there is little if anything of the wild, untamed beauty of the Atami Museum example (Plate 8). In its place we have a graceful, even voluptuous beauty, wearing a fashionable kimono with a tasteful design. There is little here to remind the viewer of the miserable existence that such women, the lowest class of prostitutes, must have eked out. The pose of the figure is as charming as its engaging smile, with a kind of emotional appeal that is rare in Japanese genre painting.

99. A "KAMBUN BEAUTY"
Coll. Ujiie Takeo
Colors on paper. Two panels, of which only one shown; 66.0 × 29.1 cm.

Another small panel showing a so-called "Kambun-period beauty" (see Plate 92, above); here the figure is holding a stalk of flowering peony and sitting, oddly enough, in a chair. The panel is an extremely rare example among others of its kind, for in almost all the others the subject is shown standing, usually as if midway in a dance. Still, even this unusual type of composition seems to have had its imitators and mass producers, for a number of fairly obvious copies are known.

100. DANCING COURTESAN ?
Coll. Tokyo National Museum
Colors on paper. Single panel; 80.3 × 25.2 cm.

This delightful portrait is said to be another example of the "Kambun beauty," (Plate 92) this time caught by the painter in an action-filled moment from a dance, one hand holding a fan raised level with the performer's head. Technically, the woman shown is traditionally identified as a *shirabyoshi*, a designation for professional female dancers who combined prostitution with their art and are known under this term from at least the twelfth century. From the first part of the seventeenth century on the term again came into vogue, designating, along with "bath women" and many other kinds of curiously named harlots, one of the many varieties of officially condoned prostitutes who flourished in the growing cities of early feudal Japan.

To the present author, however, this identification seems out of keeping with the fashionable costume, with its pattern of plantain leaves scattered over its surface, and also out of harmony with the evident beauty of the dancer pictured. Rather it would seem more suitable to identify the subject of this panel as one of the male impersonators of the early Kabuki stage. Such male dancers were extremely popular in the seventeenth and eighteenth centuries not only on stage but also as homosexual prostitutes, and in both of these roles they often served as subjects for genre painting.

101. MALE DANCER
Coll. Atami Museum of Fine Art
Colors on paper. Single panel; 92.12 × 35.15 cm.

The dancer pictured is probably a female impersonator from the early Kabuki stage; he wears an elaborate kimono containing, among other decorative devices, the large characters for "autumn moon" in a cartouche. These male dancers of seventeen or eighteen were selected primarily for their physical attractions and were customarily sought after by homosexual society of the day, which led to the government decree that they to some extent disfigure themselves by shaving their forelocks.

In an attempt partially to conceal this disfigurement the actors in turn took to wearing colorful turbans on the stage, or as here, elaborate headdresses of flowers and other ornaments, which would clearly distract attention from their loss.

102. OKUMURA MASANOBU: THE OGURA MOUNTAIN VILLA
Coll. Tokyo National Museum
Colors on paper. Single panel; 32.1 × 48.5 cm.

Okumura Masanobu (1686–1764) was a student of Torii Kiyonobu, the genre master, who later went on to develop an independent style of his own. As the proprietor of a wholesale shop handling prints and printed books he devoted much of his energies to mastering the techniques of print making, and it is especially his contributions in this field which are most memorable.

In addition, however, he also produced considerable amounts of painting, and during the period from 1716 to 1755 he was certainly one of the most important artists active.

The work illustrated purports to show the Ogura Mountain Villa of the nobleman Fujiwara Sadaie; it was in this retreat that Sadaie selected from among existing Japanese poetry one poem by each of a hundred poets beginning with Emperor Tenji (626–71), and gathered them into the collection known as the *Hyakunin Isshu*. Its composition is anachronistic in the extreme, but it was a favorite trick for the later print artists to, as here, arrange classical themes in the terms of *ukiyo-e* conventions. The characters over the open porch of the tiny retreat identify it as the Ogura Mountain Villa.

103. HISHIKAWA MORONOBU: BEAUTY LOOKING OVER HER SHOULDER
Coll. Tokyo National Museum
Colors on paper. Single panel; 63.0×31.2 cm.

Hishikawa Moronobu (1618–94), known today as one of the founders of the art of the *ukiyo-e*, was born into a family of embroiderers in modern Chiba Prefecture, but came up to Edo at an early age, where he studied painting in both the Kano- and Tosa- school traditions. Naturally, he drew considerably upon the classical resources of both these schools in his work of developing the essentially plebeian art of the *ukiyo-e*. In addition to his many prints and illustrated books a considerable-number of paintings by him also survive, among which the example illustrated is surely the most remarkable.

In later years Moronobu took holy orders and styled himself Yuchiku, "Friend of the Bamboo"; since the work illustrated is signed with this name it probably dates from fairly late in his career. It shows a woman walking alone who pauses to turn and look back, and has been executed with a strikingly clean line and an impressive use of color.

104. TORII KIYONOBU: BEAUTY WITH UMBRELLA
Coll. Tokyo National Museum
Colors on paper. Single panel. 52.4×27.3 cm.

Torii Kiyonobu (1664–1729) was the founder of the Torii line of genre artists which in time came to enjoy a virtual monopoly on the production of prints showing Kabuki actors. Such works often served as bill posters for stage productions. Prints in the Torii tradition are often characterized by the Japanese as showing "feet like gourds and lines like earth worms," an apt expression for their distinctive line.

Here, as often in the considerable number of paintings known from Kiyonobu's brush, there is much to remind us of the distinctive touches of the actor prints for which his line was famous, including of course the unmistakable stance of the standing figure. This strong flavor of the actor print is sufficient to distinguish the work illustrated from many otherwise similar paintings.

The poem written on the top of the painting may be read as follows:

> *Sashikakari*
> *Kodomo no kasa wo karitareba*
> *Omoi mo yoranu*
> *Nure onna kana*
> By chance she borrowed
> A child's umbrella,
> And now finds herself
> Splattered with rain!
> (An appealing young lady!)

This is probably a mildly satirical verse added by some other hand, as a comment upon the absurdly small umbrella with which Kiyonobu has here equipped his figure. The term *nure onna* in the last line may be interpreted literally as "wet woman," but it is also commonly used to mean "appealing woman."

105. NISHIKAWA SUKENOBU: BEAUTY AT HER TOILET
Coll. Atami Museum of Fine Art
Colors on paper. Single panel; 89.39×45.15 cm.

The work illustrated is from the brush of the Kyoto *ukiyo-e*

painter Nishikawa Sukenobu (1671–1751). The *ukiyo-e* was very much an Edo product, and Kyoto artists seldom worked on it in large numbers, but the work of Sukenobu is an exception to this general statement.

The half nude figure shown busy at her mirror has just come from her bath, and the artist has cleverly caught the intentness with which she now sets about the serious business of her make-up. Japanese artists of the time, however, must be admitted to have been sadly out of their element when dealing with the undraped female form. Their lack of practice in dealing with such themes accounts for the curious malformations with which, as for example the right arm in the present picture, they sometimes burdened their beauties. But the folds of the kimono are, as if by contrast, as well done as could be wished; somehow Japanese painters of the period found cloth far easier to deal with than undraped flesh.

106. TOSEN-DO RIFU: STANDING BEAUTY
Coll. Tokyo National Museum
Colors on paper. Single panel; 102.1×41.5 cm.

The work illustrated depends for its main effect on the contrast of the black upper garment with the red kimono underneath. The striking pose of the female figure is of course that of the "Kaigetsu-do beauty" (see the caption to Plate 10), and although the artist, Tosen-do Rifu, is a completely undocumented figure in Japanese art, it is reasonable to assume that he was working in the traditions of the school of Kaigetsu-do Ando. Here it is easy to see how closely his work conformed to the canons of this school. The work illustrated is thought to date from about 1730.

107. MIYAGAWA CHOKI: COURTESAN ENJOYING INCENSE
Coll. Tokyo National Museum
Colors on paper. Single panel; 63.9×32.4 cm.

Miyagawa Choki (mid eighteenth century) was a student of Miyagawa Choshun (see Plates 108 & 109), and a painting by his master similar in composition to the one illustrated is also known. Incense had long been enjoyed in Japan, especially as a polite accomplishment for ladies, but during the Edo period (1614–1868) it became something of a fashionable rage, and appears to have been especially the vogue in the pleasure quarters of the city. Compared with the work of his master Choshun, Choki's painting is somewhat more effete, and in sense and style completely his own.

108. MIYAGAWA CHOSHUN: FEMALE FIGURE
Important Art Object. Coll. Yamato Bunka-kan
Colors on paper. Single panel; 90.5×35.0 cm.

The work illustrated is surely the masterpiece of Miyagawa Choshun, the master of Miyagawa Choki (see Plate 107). Choshun was at first a student of the style of Hishikawa Moronobu (see Plate 103), and then later came under the influence of the work of the Kaigetsu-do school (see Plate 10), but finally achieved his own independent style in about the period 1716-35. He stressed a certain enchanted, unreal beauty in the full, voluptuous beauties in which he specialized.

The painting reproduced is typical of the work of Choshun, but is nevertheless one of those in which his debt to the Kaigetsu-do school is plainly evident.

109. MIYAGAWA CHOSHUN: COURTESAN ENJOYING INCENSE
Coll. Tokyo National Museum
Colors on paper. Single panel; 87.16×36.7 cm.

A courtesan here is seen at the height of her enjoyment of the then fashionable pastime of incense burning. The fragrant substance has been ignited on a holder set on the floor near her feet. Its aromatic smoke enters her kimono at the bottom, winds its way up under her loose garments, and after being deeply inhaled escapes into the upper air from her neckline. On her face there is a look approaching ecstasy, as she half hides herself in the upper portion of her kimono, the better to drink in the fragrance. It would be difficult to imagine a scene more refined or effete.

Especially when a painting of this type is compared, for example, with the coarse, vigorous figures of the "Bath Women" (Plate 8) from the Atami Museum Collection the contrast is striking. As time went on, the courtesans of the cities became more and more elegant and cultured, and added more and more refinements and accomplishments to their trade.

110. HISHIKAWA MORONOBU: GENRE SCROLL
Coll. Tokyo National Museum
Colors on silk. Horizontal scroll; 32.1 × 697.0 cm.

Hishikawa Moronobu pioneered in producing prints dealing with scenes in the Yoshiwara, old Edo's chief licensed quarter, and the popularity of these prints with the general public was a contributing factor to the development of the art of the ukiyo-e.

The detail reproduced, although showing a street scene of the Yoshiwara, is one of a series of separate paintings centered mainly about the popular Kabuki theater which were assembled in scroll form by a celebrated collector of the Edo period. The Kabuki theater was a theme to which he turned time and time again between 1672 and 1689, and the present scroll bears eloquent testimony to his skill. The figure in the center walking to the right with a maid servant may well be an actor from the Kabuki theater, judging from his typical head dress which was commouly used to hide the shaven forelocks of Kabuki actors.

111. MIYAGAWA CHOSHUN: GENRE SCROLL
Coll. Tokyo National Museum
Colors on paper. Horizontal scroll; 37.0 × 387.8 cm.

Miyagawa Choshun (1682–1752) was a specialist in genre painting and the founder of the Miyagawa school, who was active especially around the period from 1716 to 1735. It is interesting to note that he took no part in the production of prints, one of the fashions of the day, but completely restricted his talents to painting itself.

The detail illustrated is from a scroll showing scenes connected with the inviting of a troupe of Kabuki entertainers to a command performance before a feudal dignitary. The entire work, executed in heavy colors, shows street scenes in Edo with flowering plum trees, ladies of high position watching a dance performed by the invited troupe of entertainers, and the Kabuki greenroom.

Persons of high station during the feudal period were sometimes not content with the performances they could witness in the public theaters, and often appear to have enjoyed such private spectacles, somewhat as a tribute to their rank and position. It is unusual to find a genre scene from this period devoted, as this one is, to the activities of the upper classes.

112–15. IWASA KATSUMOCHI: THE THIRTY-SIX POETS
Important Cultural Property. Coll. Tosho-gu
Colors on wood. Thirty-six panels; each panel 47.57 × 30.30 cm.

It had long been traditional in Japan to consider that the painter Iwasa Matahei was the founder of the art of the ukiyo-e, but with the discovery in 1897 of the set of paintings from which four are reproduced here, this thesis became untenable. Among the panels

of this set were found two bearing an inscription, dating them in correspondence with 1640, and signed "By Katsumochi, Iwasa Matahei, of the school of Tosa Mitsunobu." This made it clear that Iwasa Matahei had worked in the Tosa school tradition, and that he had signed his work with the name Katsumochi.

Study of all known paintings signed with the distinctive circular seal of Katsumochi soon revealed that among them not a single ukiyo-e was to be found; all the work of Katsumochi appears to have been devoted to portraits of poets or to Chinese subject matter.

Because of this, the set from which four panels are reproduced has exceptional value for the study of the career of Iwasa Matahei, and for the proper evaluation of his position in the history of Japanese painting. Illustrated are, from upper left, Ono no Komachi, the ideal of feminine beauty, the courtier Narihira, the poetess Ise, and the poet Kakinomoto no Hitomaro.

116. THE HORIE ROMANCE SCROLL
Coll. Atami Museum of Fine Art
Colors on paper. Horizontal scroll; 35.15 cm. wide

The detail illustrated is from a scroll devoted to The Horie Romance, a story which appeared in the early years of the Edo period (1614–1868). The extremely beautiful daughter of the wealthy Hara family marries Horie Yorizumi, a warrior, by whom she has a son Tsukiwaka. Following his father's death Horie is reduced to abject poverty, and the greedy Hara attempts to force his daughter to leave her husband.

Both daughter and husband as a result commit suicide; but their son is rescued by his wet nurse, and after he grows up he sets out to avenge his parents upon the Hara family. Thus the picture scroll illustrated is largely devoted to the tales of feudal vendetta and revenge so popular among the warrior class in feudal Japan. In style it closely resembles the scroll of which a portion is illustrated in Plate 117, and although it is attributed to Iwasa Katsumochi, this attribution is probably not to be maintained.

117. LADY TOKIWA SCROLL
Coll. Atami Museum of Fine Art
Colors on paper. Horizontal scroll; 34.5 cm. wide

The scroll of which a section is reproduced here is a long work devoted to the legendary adventures of the young Minamoto Yoshitsune, at the time still using his childhood name of Ushiwakamaru. His mother, Lady Tokiwa, sets out with a few ladies-in-waiting to visit her son, but is set upon by brigands in the mountains and slain. The young Yoshitsune learns of her fate and after many hardships succeeds in avenging her death upon her killers.

The present scroll is distinguished for its heavy, thick coloration, as well as for its exceptional clarity of detail and effective use of exaggeration for dramatic and narrative effect. This scroll, too, has long been attributed to the brush of Iwasa Matahei, but again the attribution is far from certain; in the present case, however, the execution of the faces of the figures is somewhat in favor of his authorship. The painting most likely dates from the early part of the Edo period (1614–1868); the story which it tells was popular at this time, and was often performed by marionette shows.

118. THE OGURI HANGAN ROMANCE SCROLL
Coll. The Imperial Family
Colors on paper. Horizontal scroll; 33.9 cm. wide

An involved Buddhist didactic romance of the early Edo period (1614–1868) is the narrative to which the scroll of which a portion is reproduced here is devoted. Oguri Hangan is a powerful figure who suddenly finds himself reduced to helplessness and exile. In his exile he meets a Princess Terute, but is slain by her people. The princess is in turn sent into exile herself, where she endures many hardships, while the dead Oguri is permitted by the King of the Underworld to return to life as a reincarnated spirit because of the good merit which he accumulated while still on earth. In this incarnation he is able to effect a reunion with the princess.

The style resembles that of the scrolls reproduced in Plates 116 and 117, but once again the traditional attribution to Iwasa Matahei is not easily accepted. Here also we can observe that in the narrative techniques of such scrolls, a certain banality and commonplace quality had by this time begun to set in.

119. THE PRINCESS JORURI ROMANCE SCROLL

Coll. Atami Museum of Fine Art

Colors on paper. Horizontal scroll; 33.9 cm. wide

The romance dealing with Princess Joruri ("Pure Crystal") appears to have been current in Japan from the middle of the Muromachi period (1333–1573) on. The young Minamoto Yoshitsune meets Princess Joruri in the course of his adventures, and plights his troth to her. Later when he is taken ill it is the princess who nurses him back to health and makes it possible for him to continue his campaigns.

The picture scroll from which a detail is illustrated here is notable for its beautifully detailed expression, and is extremely close in style to that seen in Plate 117. Again, the attribution to Iwasa Matahei must not be taken too seriously; it is more correct probably to see behind all these scrolls the work of a special group of journeymen painters who devoted themselves to this particular style.